Genderstanding Jesus

Women in His View

For: Donia,

Meryl James-Sebro, Ph.D.

Love + Blessings,

Meryl J. Sebro

6/18/06

TEACH Services, Inc.
New York

2005 06 07 08 09 10 11 12 · 5 4 3 2 1

Copyright © 2003 Meryl James-Sebro
TXu1-112-032 / July 7, 2003
Copyright © 2005 Meryl James-Sebro and TEACH
Services, Inc.
ISBN-13: 978-1-57258-324-5
ISBN-10: 1-57258-324-X
Library of Congress Control Number: 2005927775

Published by

TEACH Services, Inc.
www.TEACHServices.com

Trust in the Lord with all your heart;
And lean not unto your own understanding.
In all your ways acknowledge Him;
And He shall direct your paths.

—Proverbs 3:5–6

DEDICATION

This book is dedicated to my grandmother, Lavinia McNellie-St.Hill, who introduced me to Jesus Christ; my mother, Sybil Olga James, who nurtured the relationship; and to "Teacher" Merle Look Loy, who guided me to a deeper relationship with Him. Hallelujah!

CONTENTS

FOREWORD

"Women Arise"
by Leith H. Dunn, Ph.D.[1]

'Genderstanding Jesus unearths the love of a faithful Father for His daughters. It is a call to women to understand, continue and reaffirm the work that only they can do. It seeks to clarify the misunderstandings about gender relations in the Bible.' (p7–8)

God's love for women shines through Meryl James-Sebro's book, which provides insight and analysis of gender relations in the Bible. *Genderstanding* **Jesus** takes us on a journey, enables us to look at women through Jesus' eyes, using the model of His life, His Ministry and His Message to bring harmony and equality to human relations. It highlights gender biases in the interpretation of many Bible stories, which she notes, are the source of unequal power relations between men and women, gender-based violence and persistent inequality. With characteristic humour, and in clear and simple language, James-Sebro convincingly demonstrates that Jesus broke through social and religious barriers to empower women. He consistently used them in His service to transform society and spread His Good News. This leadership role

---

1   Dr. Leith Dunn is an international development and gender specialist, based in Jamaica, W.I.

for women contrasts sharply with the subordinate roles traditionally ascribed to them.

Divinely guided, *Genderstanding* **Jesus** educates, inspires and challenges readers to search for wholeness and harmony in human relationships. This journey starts with an introduction to women of substance in the Bible. James-Sebro raises the veil of invisibility, suspicion and doubt, traditionally associated with women, and demonstrates through their lives how Jesus elevated them to leadership positions, using them as evangelists and missionaries in 'Kingdom building.' With conviction, she shows that Jesus freed women from traditional, subordinate roles in society and the Church. He empowered women to embrace the diversity of God's gifts, to become good stewards and to follow the Holy Spirit. Women are challenged to transform and change society through greater participation in the building of God's Kingdom.

Genderstanding **Jesus** also represents solid academic scholarship, based on systematic research of Bible Scriptures, documentary reviews, and interviews with powerful "women of the cloth." The powerful testimonies of these women who have broken the 'glass ceiling' to become church leaders, challenges Christians and congregations to revise their traditional interpretations of Bible scriptures and Church structures to embrace the full potential which the Gospel of Jesus provides to all people.

Applying gender analytical tools to the Scriptures, the roles of men and women in the Bible come to life, sharpened by James-Sebro's extraordinary skill as a Caribbean storyteller. Old and New Testament characters become contemporary human beings with whom the reader can easily relate. Her frank, incisive humour cuts through the text to reveal powerful everyday personalities.

There is the Adam and Eve story, in which both have sinned equally, but Adam blames Eve for causing him to 'fall'. Traditional interpretation of Eve's role has left women a legacy of blame and consequent subordination, in spite of God's expressed intention to use woman to crush the source of evil:

> *And I will put enmity between thee and the woman, and between thy seed and her seed; it shall bruise thy head, and thou shalt bruise his heel."* **(Genesis 3:15, KJV)**

James-Sebro contrasts the negative portrayal of Eve with the powerful position given to women through Mary, showing that, as promised, 'God chose woman as the vessel through which He would send His Son, the Saviour.' Her vivid portrayal of Mary, the unmarried pregnant teenager, *insisting* that she is a virgin, amidst the criticisms and suspicions of her strict society, but emerging triumphant as the mother of Jesus, is a powerful symbol of women's Divinely assigned co-leadership.

James-Sebro extracts case studies of strong, faithful *'Break through women'* in the Bible, and demonstrates that Jesus understood and responded to the women's basic needs. She explores several themes and issues affecting women. Poverty (the widow's mite), temptation (the woman stoned for adultery), menstruation problems (the woman with the issue of blood), menopause (the woman with the infirmity) and loneliness (the widow burying her son). These New Testament stories show women emerging triumphant because of their faithfulness, determination and commitment to God and remind us that God cares and forgives His daughters, even when they transgress. Moreover, He shows up in the midst of the most hopeless situations.

Genderstanding **Jesus** then introduces *'No turning back women'* and *'women of substance'* who 'stand firm' despite the challenges of their society. It challenges women to get 'Out of the Kitchen' (their traditional roles), and to equip themselves by understanding the Word to become agents of change, regardless of the obstacles and hardships this implies. It encourages women to make time to qualify themselves for this purpose, and to stay focussed and vigilant, in the face of distraction, discouragement and fear.

Genderstanding **Jesus** provides a channel for spiritual reflection on issues rarely covered and often difficult to discuss. It is thought-provoking, reminding us of the hope and the possibility of salvation for even the worst sinners.

It will be of use to a wide range of readers. The general public will find it easy to read and understand. No doubt, theologians will find it enlightening, and Ministers of Religion will explore the themes and issues for their sermons. Congregations and Christian educators will find it a useful resource for Christian Stewardship programmes, as well as use it to develop Bible Study materials for children, adolescents and adults. Gender specialists will gain insight from examining how gender analysis has been used to analyze Scriptures. Leaders of churches and Theological institutions can use the book for policy analysis and development in relation to the role and position of women in the church.

Women who want to offer themselves for service will feel empowered and encouraged to search the scriptures more carefully. Church historians will be encouraged to excavate the context in which many positions on women were developed in order to better understand them. For example, the book provides an explanation of the scripture which says that women should be silent in church. James-Sebro also provides questions for reflection at the end of each chapter. These enhance the educational role to which the text can be used, and provide discussion material for women's groups and youth groups.

The author, Meryl James-Sebro, is a strong committed Christian, a feminist anthropologist and a Caribbean woman, whose writing and storytelling skills translate complex issues and events into everyday reality. It is a singular honour to have been asked to write the Foreword for this exciting publication. I have been richly blessed by its reading, and I have no doubt that readers will be similarly blessed and moved to inspired, Spirit-led action.

Leith L. Dunn, Ph.D.
Jamaica, W.I.

ACKNOWLEDGEMENTS

When you initiate serious Heavenly dialogue about His Plan and Purpose for your life, there is need for complete surrender to the Holy Spirit, an act with particularly surprising challenges for women. The writing of this book is the result of this surrender and consequent guidance in response to the Divine command: "Go, Write!"

The subject matter was easy, given my own passions about women's issues and my increasing frustration with the marginalized position of women in the Church. My work with women, particularly research on domestic violence, highlighted questions and concerns about insensitivity to women's issues, especially when women turned to the Church as their only source of help. More troubling, is the apparent contradiction between gender equality, justice and stock Christianity, which, for many feminist activists, prevents the link between spirituality and empowerment. An exploration of these issues with Margaret Neckles of Grenada triggered my vow to look more closely at the ways in which Jesus Christ interacted with women in the New Testament, and sharpened my commitment to write about it. Margaret would be the first of the many angels to help forward this project.

Soon after I re-visited the Woman at the Well. Through new eyes, I saw her mission as a more action-oriented model for the participation of Christian women. A model which, in my view was being sidelined. I shared my observations one Thanksgiving with Dr. Walter Douglas, Chair of the Church History Department at Andrews University in Michigan, USA, and he gave me a capsulized version of the messianic mission of the Woman at the Well. When I casually mentioned my intention of doing a book on the subject, I was surprised and encouraged by his enthusiasm and excitement. Dr. Patrick Alleyne and Dr. Leith Dunn had similar responses that fueled my intention and energy in the earliest stages of this writing. Leith was one of three readers who helped to edit the first draft, and she kindly agreed to present her analysis in the preceding Foreword. Pastor Brenda Billingy was the second reader. I joke that the Lord either thought me particularly problematic or extra-special to have blessed me with the sister-love and friendship of this powerful "woman of the cloth." Sister Pastor, I call her. So even before her interview, reading and comments on the manuscript, she was and continues to be my spiritual consultant, prayer warrior and front-line cheerleader.

The third reader was Dr. Hyveth Williams, another dynamic pastor, who has become a treasured sister through the writing of this book. Her personal style, spiritual depth and an iconoclasm that is grounded and shaped in His Love, Wisdom and Power, boosted my own confidence and strengthened my sense of purpose and mission. I am indebted to her for more than her support and encouragement of this work through her reading of the manuscript and generous sharing of her sermon, "Where Eagles Fly," as an Afterword. More than ever, I am grateful for the trails she is painfully blazing for those courageous women who are called to be endtime "battle axes" for God.

There were other "women of the cloth" to whom I was Divinely led, and whose voices and experiences shape, validate and bring a deeper understanding to this book: Pastor Lucille Baird (Barbados); Pastor Paula Olivier (New Jersey) Pastor Annette Taylor (Liberia/Maryland). Pastor Grace Philip of Agape Bible Ministries (Trinidad and

Tobago) and my West African sister, Clavender Bright-Parker (Liberia/Ghana/Maryland) were invaluable guides. There were writer/scholar friends: Joy Elliott, Audrey Edwards, Althea Kironde-Lee, Dr. Yvonne Bobb-Smith and my American University tea-liming, anthropologist 'sistahs' who encouraged and cheered; and Professor Acklyn Lynch, whose incisive questioning on a BWEE flight pushed me to expand a chapter. My sister, Beverly James, Norma Shorey-Bryan and her sister, Denise, supplied timely research material; and my stepson Anthony Sebro, Jr. provided, as always, thought-provoking criticism. Denyse Matthew and Bena Riley rendered over-the-top assistance and support, and Dawn and Josh Wout and Yolande Joseph gave cover design guidance.

But it is my husband, Anthony Sebro, Sr., who not only lived gracefully with my many neuroses during this writing, but challenged many issues that led to greater clarification and refinement. This, then, has been a work of Spirit-guided collaboration, and I give Him All Glory and Praise. Mere expressions of gratitude are inadequate to every one of these "book angels" and those I may have neglected to mention. May your paths be showered with His love, light, joy, presence, peace, prosperity and power...and, to borrow the words of the Psalmist:

May the favour of the Lord our God rest upon us; establish the work of our hands for us. Yes, establish the work of our hands. *(Psalm 90:17, NIV)*

MJ-S

Chapter 1

INTRODUCTION

At church one day in 1994, the pastor used the pulpit to educate the congregation on the alleged evils of feminism. "Feminism is of the devil," he pronounced. This took place a few months before the United Nations Fourth World Conference of Women in Beijing, and women all over the world—in particular women from developing countries—were in feverish preparation, strategizing, planning, begging, borrowing and raising funds, prodding unenlightened governments to support their agendas of equality: development, peace, justice and human rights for all. Even though I had not been planning to attend the Beijing conference, my own work as a development anthropologist/consultant had kept me peripherally involved in the preparation. Needless to say, as a Christian feminist, I was stunned beyond consolation. The comparative youth of the pastor (he appeared to be under 40) was cause for even greater consternation.

At the end of the church service, I introduced myself to the pastor at the door, and politely explained that I was a Christian feminist, involved in applying feminist analyses to government policies and programmes, i.e. gender equality and women's participation in decision-making at the highest levels. If indeed I was participating in work of the devil, I wanted to be educated so that I could beg forgiveness and change my evil ways. If he were privy to information that I didn't have, I wanted him to give me the heads-up.

Politely, he handed me his card, and suggested that I call for discussion at a more opportune time. It took several instances of telephone tag to connect, and when we finally did, I attempted to explain the concept of feminism. After all, the Oxford Dictionary describes feminism as "advocacy of women's rights on grounds of equality of the sexes," and the Webster New World Dictionary calls it "the movement to win political, economic and social equality for women." Caribbean scholar/writer Rhoda Reddock describes it more succinctly as: "the awareness of the subordination of women and the conscious action to change the situation."[2] What on earth could be evil about that? On the contrary, I clearly saw a Christian imperative.

Undaunted, the pastor launched into the evils of lesbianism. But lesbianism is by no means synonymous with feminism, I argued. Yes, it is an extreme feminist position, and one which, as a Christian woman, I certainly did not then and do not now condone. The feminism to which I subscribe and which I defended in our conversation focused on the liberation of women from their structural subordination—socially, culturally, economically, politically, with strong "religious" support of this subordination, intentional or not. It is this structural subordination that has doomed women to a life of inequality, and negatively impacted their own development, the development of their families, and by extension whole societies, global development and peace. In fact global development activists have linked the elimination of poverty to the empowerment of women economially, socially and politically. Interestingly, Christian feminist activists, linking the personal and political to the spiritual, have begun to question the failure of development programmes to connect and include women's spirituality, and to stress the

---

2   "Caribbean Feminism at the Turn of the Century: Introductory Remarks," in Women, Globalisation and Fair Trade. *Cafra News* 16 (July-December 2002).

importance of spiritual development to the success of development programmes.

On the other hand, most feminists draw our attention to the negative impact of fundamentalism on women worldwide, particularly in the major religions, including Christianity and Islam. They point to the control mechanisms embedded in these systems to maintain power through the control of women's economic independence and sexuality, a control in which violence—physical, emotional, psychological, financial and religious—is rooted. When we truly unearth the connection between overt and covert violence against women and the ripple effects of violence in our society, we see an unbroken chain that joins incest, child abuse, rape, sexual harassment in the workplace, increasing violence against women in the workplace, economic violence against women, political exclusion in their countries and general societal dysfunction.

The tragic events of "Nine-Eleven" have front-lined and dramatized the plight of the Afghanistani women, and indeed the extraordinary evil of this structural subordination of women. More significantly, it points to the link between women's rights and human security. In the words of UNDP programme administrator, Mark Malloch Brown: "What has happened to women in Afghanistan demonstrated that if a country or community fails to treat women well and protect and promote their human rights this is one of the best early warning indicators of the lack of respect for international norms and standards."[3] Indeed the international feminist movement had been waging a cyberspace protest, more than a decade before that fateful September day in 2001, collecting signatures via the Internet to inform the world and bring aid to the women of Afghanistan. But my 1994 conversation with the esteemed pastor had occurred during the previous innocence of

---

3   "Women's Rights and Human Security," *Choices* (New York: United Nations Development Programme, March 2002).

ignorance and wide-spread male insensitivity to the plight of women and the poor globally, and poor women from so-called developing countries in particular. Practices such as female genital mutilation, more widely understood as female circumcision; traditions such as *sati* in India that require a widow to burn herself to death on the pyre of her deceased husband; and the fact that domestic violence may be the leading cause of injury and death to women worldwide[4]; dowry-related deaths, dowry harassment, wife battery and "honour killings"; female infanticide and sex-selected abortion because of the societal preference for boys; the selling of girls from poor families to pay off debts; the preferential care and feeding of boys, all escaped our gaze. Worldwide, **one** out of **three** women is a victim of domestic violence. All of these uglies were too far away; too bizarre; beyond our, comprehension; not seen on CNN or Oprah.[5]

In the West we tended to focus on middle-class feminists who struggled for equal pay for equal work, day-care centers that enabled the care of children to allow mothers—both single and married—to pursue desired careers; sexual harassment in the workplace; the big, vexatious issue of abortion or choice; and the sexual division of labour, both in the home and the outside world, all the while demonizing the women who were in the forefront of these struggles. We forgot, however, communities of African-American and other Diaspora Africans, Latin Americans, Asian Americans and poor white Americans (the so-called "Third World" in the belly of the so-called "First World"), who are experiencing tremendous vulnerability that makes us easy targets of racial, gender, social and economic discrimination. Gender-based violence is now recognized worldwide as a

---

4   J. Seager, *The State of Women in the World Atlas* (Penguin: London, 1997).
5   To their credit, both CNN and "The Oprah Winfrey Show" have since provided coverage on gender-based violence.

critical development issue, a major public health concern and a fundamental violation of women's human rights.

Statistics of violent deaths of women and children within the sanctity of their homes by some physically powerful male have crossed barriers of class, ethnicity, age and national origin and escaped the conspiracy of silence to assault our senses and disturb our "couch-potato" comfort on the evening news. The facts are not pretty: In[6] the United States and Canada, 31% of all women killed are murdered by their husbands, ex-spouses or boyfriends. Violence occurs in 28% of all marriages. Recently Domestic Violence has been recognized as the Number One health threat to U.S. women, causing more injuries than automobile accidents, muggings and rapes combined. And while domestic violence indeed includes violence against men, according to the U.S. Department of Justice, 85% of victims of intimate partner abuse are female. Moreover, a recent American Medical Association (AMA) study revealed that the cost of family violence in the U.S. is $5 billion annually, related to medical expenses, police and court costs, and loss of productivity in the work place. Ugly stuff.

In fact, Pastor Annette Taylor of Liberia, founder and president of The Shepherd Ministry International which ministers to pastors and gospel workers, observes: "I find that in the Body of Christ, women are more suppressed in the United States of America than even in Africa." We close our ears to the fact that in the United States, every fifteen seconds a woman is beaten by her husband or boyfriend. Around the world, **one** out of **three** women has been beaten, coerced into sex or otherwise abused in her lifetime. The abuser is frequently a member of her own family. It is important to see how these social and economic issues have become well-entrenched obstacles

---

6   Leni Marin, Helen Zia and Esta Soler, ed., *Ending Domestic Violence: Report From the Global Frontlines* (San Francisco, California: The Family Violence Prevention Fund).

to women's realization of their full potential, thus blocking full participation in their societies. Human kind continues to reap the cost in a violence and disconnect that is growing in intensity and prevalence. At the same time we stubbornly fail to connect the plight of women to a skill-fully-contrived, all-powerful male that Biblical scholars and other religious interpreters had defined and promoted to support a chauvinist Divinity, bent on punishing Eve and her hapless daughters for all eternity.

Now talk to me, Brother Pastor. To his credit, the pastor listened intently, argued some, then surprisingly agreed and apologized. Admittedly, it was extremely gracious of him. But the damage had been already done; and I had been searching, not for an apology, but for a recognition of the degree to which the Church was out of sync with the realities of women's lives, and how glibly and self-assur-edly ignorance was promoted. He had already infected an entire congregation with anti-feminist propaganda that he attributed to satan. In part he was right, because this struc-tural subordination of women that is reflected in the pervasive discrimination of women in society, and the marginalizing of women in the Christian church is a divisive strategy that comes live and direct from the bowels of hell. But we shouldn't be surprised, because we have been forewarned that:

> *we wrestle not against flesh and blood, but against principalities, against powers, against the rulers of the darkness of this world, against spiritual wickedness in high places.* **(Ephesians 6:12, KJV)**

The carnal effects are extreme in the linkage of women's inequality to all forms of gender-based violence. The Fourth World Conference on Women in 1995 observed that "poverty has a woman's face," and wrote a number on that face. The number 70. Women represent 70 percent of the world's poor. And this poverty is a direct result of women's lack of economic opportunities to support themselves and their families, spawned, as mentioned before, from the structural subordination of women in almost all societies. In an address upon receiving an honorary doctorate from the University of Cape Town, United Nations Secretary-General Kofi Annan said: "Women make up 50 percent of the global AIDS epidemic—and in Africa that figure is now 58 per cent. Today, AIDS has a woman's face." Health researchers are now making a link between domestic violence and the spread of HIV/AIDS among women, given their subordination and economic and emotional dependence on those who victimize them. In a later address, the Secretary-General warned that the future of the world depends on women.

The good news, however, is that Jesus broke through social, cultural and religious traditions to exonerate and empower women. The Bible itself offers awesome examples of women who followed His lead, and with His full support and approval, broke societal barriers. "Break-Through Women," they're called by Pastor Lucille Baird of Mt. Zion Ministries in Barbados, West Indies.

A "Break-Through Woman" herself, Pastor Baird describes herself as "a mighty woman of God; a nation builder," taking her direction from Genesis 1:26–28.

> And God said, Let us make man in our image, after our likeness; and let **them** have dominion over the fish of the sea, and over the fowl of the air, and over the cattle, and over all the earth, and over every creeping thing that creepeth upon the earth. So God created man in His own image, in the image of God created He him; male and female created He **them**. And God blessed **them**, and God said unto **them**, Be fruitful, and multiply, and replenish the earth, and subdue it: and have dominion over the fish of the sea, and over the fowl of the air, and over every living thing that moveth upon the earth.

Genderstanding **Jesus** unearths the love of a faithful Father for His daughters. It points to the many ways in which Jesus empathized with women's subjugation and suffering. Moreover, He drew them out of the crowds to validate and display their faith as object lessons, and to use them in front-line positions for the spread of His Message. *Genderstanding* **Jesus** becomes a clarion call to women to understand, accept, reaffirm and continue the work that only they can do. But first, there is a need to listen, to hear and to answer that Call. In addition, it is a reminder to men of the far-reaching implications of adherence to man-made traditions that not only continue to subordinate women, but subject us all to the devious, devilish and divisive wiles of the enemy. In so doing, *Genderstanding Jesus* explains, explores, reveals, and hopefully reverses some of the misunderstandings about gender relations in the Bible. Its central premise is the unmistakable love and respect with which Jesus treated women; its primary focus, the dignity and value of women, which Jesus affirmed throughout His Life. Its hope is to promote discussion within the Christian Church of the role of women in the Church, and to examine the extent to which the Church itself contributes to the structural subjugation of women, and in that context ignores the issue of domestic violence that has been plaguing the harmonious family life that the Church espouses. Moreover, it challenges the Christian community to new understanding and action, doing as Jesus did, to include, "big-up" and utilize women in the transformation of societies, and the world, to a prosperity and joy that is linked to the peace that comes from the equality of all women and men. For as none other than Paul, whose perception of the role of women many question, reminds the church of Galatians:

> *For ye are all the children of God by faith in Christ Jesus. For as many of you as have been baptized into Christ have put on Christ. There is neither Jew nor Greek, there*

is neither bond nor free, there is neither male nor female:
for ye are all one in Christ Jesus.   *(3:26-28, KJV)*

More urgently, it is a reminder to women of the critical importance of reading the Word for ourselves, allowing the Holy Spirit to interpret and to guide us to God's special intention for our unique lives, and the danger of relying on male-dominated or gender neutral interpretations. It is a responsibility we have to ourselves and to others to whom we must communicate God's special love for all humanity—women and men.

What then is *Genderstanding*? It is a full understanding of the unequal power relations between women and men, and its poisonous effects on relationships, communities, societies, the Body of Christ, human security, social and economic development and world peace. ***Genderstanding Jesus*** seeks to deconstruct and dismantle the structural and institutionalized subordination of women in contemporary Christianity. It responds to the question: What Would Jesus Do about gender relations? To ***Genderstand Jesus*** is to examine the lives of women from His View, and to use the model of His Life, His Ministry and His Message to bring equality and harmony to human relationships. Let's begin at the very beginning: Adam and Eve.

Genderstanding Jesus:
Questions for Reflection, Discussion and Action
Chapter 1

1). What do you understand by the concept of *Genderstanding*?

2). How does it relate to *Genderstanding* Jesus?

3). What is the connection between Genderstanding and gender-based violence?

4). What steps can you take to bring about greater *Genderstanding*?

5). Do you think gender-based violence is present in your church or community?

6). How can you help victims of domestic violence?

Chapter 2

...AND GOD CHOSE A WOMAN

"EVE WAS FRAMED." Thus read the bumper sticker of a shiny BMW that flashed past me, piloted by a woman as confident-looking as her car was snazzy.

It brought to mind my own constant amazement that Eve has become the whipping girl of anti-woman humanity and, by extension, Christianity. She is the source of all blame for the fall of man and woman kind, and the main reason for the lingering perception of women as creatures of suspicion, deception and temptation. Indeed it was the mother of all set-ups...a set-up that has not stopped. I was once in the midst of a group of Christians who spent a lot of time arguing over Adam's role in the temptation. Was he with Eve at the time of the temptation? Was it joint temptation, with Eve simply accepting and tasting the fruit first before passing it to Adam? The King James version states:

> *And when the woman saw that the tree was good for food, and that it was pleasant to the eyes, and a tree to be desired to make one wise, she took of the fruit thereof, and did eat, and gave also unto her husband <u>with</u> her; and he did eat.*   *(Gen 3:6 KJV)*

Or, did she take the fruit to Adam, who was in another location, as suggested by some interpretations.

> *The woman saw how good the fruit looked as the serpent ate it. Suddenly she felt a strong urge to eat it,*

11

> *too. She took a bite and instantly felt a surge of energy.*
> *Excited, she took more fruit and ran to find her husband.*
> *When Adam saw her, he knew what she had done and*
> *also what the consequences would be. But in the blush of*
> *her excitement, she looked more beautiful than ever. He*
> *couldn't bear the thought of living without her, so he*
> *quickly took the fruit and ate it also.*   *(Gen. 3:6 CWV)*

Whether Adam was there from the beginning or at the end, he was her sin-partner, and any modern day court would find him equally guilty as an accomplice. Most translations, however, advance the notion of an ever-present Adam at the moment of temptation. Yet we continue to shift the blame from the acquiescing Adam to an Eve, perceived not only as deceitful, distrustful and devious, but powerful enough to have bequeathed these innate characteristics to her descendants, selecting out her daughters for sole exclusivity. In fact, the cowardly Adam was bold enough to try to shift the blame on the Creator Himself:

> *The man said, 'The woman you put here with me—she*
> *gave me some fruit from the tree, and I ate it.'*
> *(Gen. 3:12, NIV)*

But the object lesson that persists through time is not in the superficial question of who sinned first, and whether it was a sole operator or double trouble act, but the more substantive one that is three-part:

1). Disobedience to God's law;

2). Taking direction from voices other than God's, thus prioritizing our will over His;

3). God's forgiveness, and the plan of Redemption and Restoration.

There is no gender differentiation here. As humans, we are all culpable and remain vulnerable. Notice, however, that Adam is at least a willing participant. It is this self-will that appears to have been the model for the fig-leaf cover-up executed by the Roman Catholic Church in its institutional hiding of paedophilia. Similar self-indulgence must also have guided big American conglomerates in their spinning of out-of-control corporate greed and undiluted, uncaring selfishness. Yet it is Eve who continues to inherit a bad rap, perhaps the only instance in history where there is eagerness and total commitment to giving prominence and leadership status to a woman. According to a Jewish legend, in addition to leading Eve into disobedience to God by eating the forbidden fruit, satan also seduced her. The result of this seduction, claims this legend, was "a permanent break with the Creator and the birth of Cain, who symbolized the union of Eve and the devil."[7] But the legend is based on only part of the story.

The missing element is the most important...God's unmatched and unending love. He goes to the extreme to prove this love through His Plan of Redemption. And when He wants to make a point, He does so dramatically and flamboyantly, as He did with the parting of the Red Sea. He could have chosen other methods to send His Son into the world. Jesus could have suddenly appeared in the desert or the temple. He could have emblazoned the skies, spreading majestic rays overhead, then dramatically descend to the earth. He could have appeared on the highest mountain top, brought by the proverbial stork, or discovered underneath a bundle of straw in the manger. But to show His specific plans and place for woman, God

---

7   "The Promise: God's Everlasting Covenant," *Adult Sabbath School Bible Study Guide* (Jan/Feb/Mar 2003), 15.

chose woman as the vessel through which He would send His Son, the Saviour, and accomplish His Plan. He pronounced it Himself:

> *And I will put enmity between thee and the woman, and*
> *Between thy seed and her seed; it shall bruise thy head,*
> *and Thou shall bruise his heel.* **(Gen 3:15, KJV)**

By this one act, He has indicated His Forgiveness and His Magnanimous Grace by bestowing favour on a woman. How well He knew that Eve would be the catalyst for the suspicion and resentment that would be unleashed on women, by men, but also by other women. How well He saw that women would be blamed for their own victimization. His choice of Mary as the medium through which His Son could walk this earth, crush the head of the serpent and triumph over sin is an indication of His grace and forgiveness. Moreover, both Adam and Eve received just punishments: Adam in labour through work for his daily bread; Eve in labour through childbirth. But they were both given the blessings of restoration and recreation, with **equal** responsibility for reconfiguring their social, cultural and spiritual spaces.[8] In fact, Adam rejoiced in the critical role his woman was to play in God's redemptive plan and called her Eve or "Life, " from the Hebrew word, *Havvah* or *Hawwah*.

> *Adam called his wife Eve, because she would become the*
> *mother of all human life, including the One who would*
> *break the power of sin and of death.* **(Gen 3:20, CWV)**

Yet human beings have insisted on dogging women with the misstep of Eve, and a sentence of subordination, while completely exonerating Adam. Misogynists make an erroneous connection between the words Eve and evil

---

8   My thanks to Professor Acklyn Lynch for the fine-tuning of this point.

to further support the subordination and discrimination of women, in spite of the completely different etymology of the word evil. But God, as only God can, in one fell swoop has wiped clean Eve's slate with His choice of the woman, Mary. His Son, Jesus, would have to be moulded with gentleness and kindness, steeped in beauty and grace, grounded in patience and tolerance, and shaped by forgiveness.

Obedience would have to be a guiding principle. And so He chose Mary, in whom He had packaged all of these characteristics to impart to His Son, and to serve as the primary counterpoint to Eve.

> *When Heaven's clock struck the time for God's Son to be born, He came, born of a human mother and subject to Jewish law. He came to redeem everyone who felt condemned by the law and to adopt us as sons and daughters of God.* **(Gal.4:4. CWV)**

Mary's was an important mission, so her gifts would include the ability to focus on His Purpose and Plan in the midst of the distractions, rumours and *mauvaise langue* that must have surrounded the pre-marital pregnancy of a 14 year-old Jewish girl. Her delicateness and gentleness would have had to be mixed with the strength of a lion in order to withstand the wagging tongues, the mockery and scorn heaped on her insistence, first of all, that she was a virgin, and, story of all stories, that an angel had appeared to her to announce her selection to carry the Son of God. Could you hear them now: "What on earth is that child smoking or drinking?" "The girl's gone stark, raving mad!"

Preparation for her special mission would have had to be a gift of tremendous faith to drive out fear. The fear of the consequences that faced an unmarried young girl with child. Surely she would be stoned to death. Fear of her fiancé Joseph. He himself could throw the first stone, and would be loudly acclaimed by a society that condoned such action. But instead of fear, Mary had been given a spirit of power, love, and a sound mind (*2 Timothy 1:7*). The Lord is in the business of giving <u>power</u> and <u>sound minds</u> to women, filling them with <u>love</u>, not fear. Hallelujah!

One woman had been weak-minded and deceived into sin. Her counterpoint would be imbued with <u>power</u> and <u>strength of purpose</u> to carry out her mission, through which human kind would be redeemed from sin. Clearly the Lord had a plan; and women were and are major actors in that plan. In fact, knowing that we might miss the point, He used two other women. First, there is Mary's cousin, Elizabeth, barren for many years, but He blessed her with a child so that she could become the living proof of the awesome miracle to which He had recruited Mary. One woman would give birth to the Redeemer, the other woman would bear His Precursor, preparing the hearts of men and women to receive Him (*Luke 1*). Note that because he dared to question God's plan, Zachariah, Elizabeth's husband, would be struck dumb until the birth of their son. After the birth of the Christ Child, God would use a third woman, Anna, a prophetess to announce the Redemptive purpose and power of the Baby, Jesus (*Luke 2:36-38*). Zachariah paid a price for his disbelief. The Church—and by extension the world—does not permit the full participation of women at leadership levels. Hence it does not participate fully in God's Redemption Plan and is paying a heavy price.

At the time of this writing, the Roman Catholic Church is being ravaged by a scandalous disclosure of paedophilia, homosexuality, sexual abuse and an abuse of power in an insidious and deliberate plan by the male-dominated Church to hide these sins against children and all God-loving and God-fearing people. Even in the face of blatant evidence, men who profess to represent God, dodge and hide behind fancy language and phrases, compounding these sins by their impenetrable arrogance and expert spinning of the truth. While men have no monopoly on immorality and vulnerability to sin, one cannot help but link this debacle to the minimization of feminine energy and guidance at key policy formulation and decision-making levels. Indeed the institutionalisation of a secondary role for women in the world Church has cheated humanity in ways that we are now beginning to see, and are yet to experience.

Jesus was fully aware of the importance of this <u>feminine energy,</u> and made sure to skillfully utilize it in the early spreading of His Ministry. Neither gender, class, ethnicity nor reputation would thwart His plan. In fact, His strategy, and His message were deliberately and strategically all-inclusive. He sent His disciples to buy food, and sat at the well in Sychar, waiting for the Samarian woman. How well we know the story! Or, more accurately, how well we **think** we know the story! He asked her for a drink of water, she queried His agenda…a Jew asking a Samarian woman for a drink of water? Socially unacceptable, breaking all of the customs and traditions of the day. He responded that if she really knew who He was, she would ask and receive the water of life itself. She persists in questioning Him, and then, convinced that He indeed had some magic, asks for this living water, if only to prevent frequent return trips to the well to face the accusing stares and gossiping tongues of the other village women. Intent on *sussing*[9] her out and testing her, Jesus invites her to bring her husband, so that they could both benefit from this magic water. "I have no husband," she honestly admits.

Jesus is pleased with her <u>honesty</u> and <u>truthfulness</u>, and then He does three things. First, He gives her the 411 on

---

9   A Jamaican colloquialism that means careful examination.

herself, demonstrating that He knows even more than she cares to admit. And it's not pretty. In fact, it's pure dirt! She is an adulteress of note, living in sin at the very moment. Unflinching, the woman "fesses" up by asking whether He is a prophet.

Secondly, he takes her through a long admonition that points to the folly of following blind traditions while neglecting the true worship of God. In so doing, He stages a frontal attack on gender, class and ethnic divisions that subjected this woman to second-class citizenship and to the structural subordination that we see in the world. In response, she admits that she doesn't understand everything He's saying, but knows that the Messiah is coming, and is confident that He will tell them what is right.

Finally, Jesus makes His dramatic declaration. "**I am The Messiah**." He reveals Himself and His Mission to her...a woman...a second-class citizen...a woman of ill repute. "**I am the Messiah**," He announces for the first time...not in the temple among religious scholars and leaders, not in the middle of one of His dramatic healing miracles, but sitting at a well, waiting for some water from an ordinary dreg of society. But, under Divine manners, Jesus came with a Plan, and He was working His Plan. He knew, understood and appreciated the talents and skills of women, and He was not going to permit societal traditions to hinder Him from efficiently utilizing those skills. Who can share good news like a woman? And so the woman runs back to the village to tell the story of her experiences with the stranger. But even more poignantly, she is careful to add: "I think He's The Messiah." or, as the King James Version says:

Is not this the Christ? *(John 4:29).*

18

According to the Clear Word Version:

> *Their curiosity was aroused by what the woman told them, and large crowds came out to see Him. (John 4:30)*

Mission accomplished! Not only did Jesus formally announce and publicize His Mission, but He overturned and transformed this woman's life from one who sought men for adulterous relationships, to one who brought men to seek Him for a spiritual relationship.[10] Her response was immediate and focused. There was no hesitation. She dropped her water pot, forgot about her own mission and went about His business. Her priorities were in place, so she enjoyed the blessing of being the first to help spread the gospel, and her community the blessing of being the first to benefit from His teaching. Herein lies a powerful message about the disadvantages, even the danger of not employing all available talents and skills in the work of God. It is a danger that not only stymies the growth of the Church, but has tremendous implications for the development of the society. According to Pastor Lucille Baird:

> So if the Church is robbed, if the local church is robbed, the society is robbed and the nations are robbed on a whole, because women are not allowed to be who they would be in Christ and to fulfil their potential in Christ, and it's really sad. Therefore, the society that should be benefitting from that particular Church is not getting the full benefit of that church, because the woman in the church is not allowed to come to her full potential in Christ in the church, and therefore in the society.
>
> —Pastor Lucille Baird
> Mt. Zion Ministries
> Barbados, W.I.

---

10   Thanks to Pastor Lucille Baird of Mt. Zion Ministries in Barbados, West Indies, for this significant elucidation.

Jesus' deep discussion with the Samarian Woman at the Well, and His employment of her <u>communications skills</u> are examples of the powerful ways in which He took time and went out of His way to minister to women and to utilize them strategically. Moreover, He took great pains to value and validate them. Why then were women not among the 12 Apostles?

For some, Jesus understood the environment in which He was operating, and knew the additional difficulties and criticism that including women would have brought to His ministry, not to mention the logistical challenges of lodging women with men during their travels. His ministry had to be above scrutiny, and He had to be careful to avoid even the very appearance of sin. That is one side of the debate. Another interesting perspective positions the 12 men as His inner circle, but includes a larger group of disciples, which included women. In fact, according to another pastor, the interpretation that the disciples were only 12 men is a misreading of the scriptures.

> But the Bible also says in Acts, in Acts Chapter 1 when Jesus spoke to the disciples, and sometimes we forget, it says that before Jesus ascended into Heaven, Jesus said to them in Acts Chapter 1, don't leave Jerusalem. He spoke to the disciples—now many times when people read the scriptures, they misread the scriptures—and they think that the disciples were only 12 men. But there were 120 disciples, which included Jesus' mother, along with all the women that walked with Him. And they were in that upper room. And when Jesus said 'Don't leave until the Holy Spirit comes,' they were in the upper room when the Holy Spirit came, and they were ALL baptized with the Holy Spirit to be what? Witnesses unto Him. So the women were just as great a witness unto Jesus as the men were. And many times—conveniently it seems—people read part of the

scripture to suit their own purpose and eschew the part
that they don't want to understand.

—Pastor Annette Taylor
Bethel Outreach Ministries
Maryland, USA

What cannot be disputed, however, is that Jesus never
ignored women. In fact, He spent a lot of time with
women, ministering to them, and allowing them to minister to Him. Women were as important to His ministry as
men, not only in the daily preparation of food, lodging
spaces and other domestic duties, but in out-front roles as
examples and graphic illustrations of their worth. Often
He front-lined them as <u>over-comers,</u> a concept on which
we will expand in the next chapter. But overall, there was
little distinction between the quality of time Jesus spent
with women and with men. Although one might make the
argument—as some scholars indeed have (e.g. Underwood 2000)—that Jesus needed to spend more time
preparing the 12 men He chose as the advance guard for
the spread of His message to the ends of the earth, given
the humility challenges which most men face, then as now.
The women, some claim, received His Message immediately, acknowledged His Divinity and followed Him
without extra persuasion, primarily because the Message
of hope for the hopeless and the oppressed held particular
meaning for them because of their second-rate citizenship.

On the contrary—according to this thinking—He had to
go seek out the men and urge them to follow Him. They
argue that women, primarily because of their subordinate
and oppressed status, are clothed with a <u>greater sensitivity</u>
and <u>concern for the oppressed</u> and are already armed with
the <u>humility, compassion</u> and <u>commitment</u> required for
service. It is important to note, too, that Jesus too came
from a socially unacceptable "minority." After all, He was
born out of wedlock. He would have know the scorn and

21

sneers of so-called high society in His early days that would mould a particular connection with women as social inferiors. Moreover, He came to save sinners; to bring light where there was darkness; hope for the hopeless and joy to the grief-stricken. He kept company with those at the bottom of society; and women were definitely at the bottom.

Yet, the contemporary Church continues to, at best, downplay the roles of women. At its worst, the patriarchal arms of the Church reach into the privacy of homes to strangle women and children through domestic violence, incest and child abuse, providing Scriptural evidence and authority for the basis of their domination. While my own anthropological research on domestic violence in the Caribbean revealed many cases in which Churches indeed provided relief, succour and support for women and children fleeing abusive environments, evidence of insensitive, callous and discriminatory ecclesiastical responses—compounded by stubborn denial or "head-in-the-sand"approaches—were pervasive. Failure to utilize the energy, talents, skills and abilities of women in the Church, and the reluctance—even refusal—to value them and give them deserved recognition have indeed paved the way for the continuing structural subordination and widespread violation of women's social, economic and political rights in the wider society.

The Bible, Thank God, is replete with women who have broken through societal boundaries to gain proximity to Jesus, physically and spiritually. In some cases, Jesus met them half way; at other times, He set up the scenario Himself to make a statement and teach a lesson. What remains constant, however, is that Jesus paid a great deal of attention to these women. These "Break Through Women," their interaction with Jesus, and the lessons which He taught us through them, are critical to

Genderstanding Jesus. Let's visit with them in the next chapter.

Genderstanding Jesus:

Questions for Reflection, Discussion and Action

Chapter 2

1). Do you agree that women continue to be blamed for Eve's sin?

2). How important was the role of the Samarian woman at the well?

3). Do you think that women were among the disciples?

4). What can women do to ensure support and encourage greater participation of women at leadership levels?

5). What specific Mission have <u>you</u> been given...individually and/or corporately?

6). What special gifts have you been given to carry out this Mission?

7). What lessons have you learnt from this Chapter?

Chapter 3

BREAK-THROUGH WOMEN

Contrary to popular world belief systems, women are not innately inferior to men. Hello! When God in His caring and thoughtfulness intended a companion for man, He said to Himself:

> *...It is not good that the man should be alone; I will make him a help meet for him.* **(Genesis 2:18, KJV)**

That is to say He created a woman, equal in status and intellect, who could be a suitable companion to share and enjoy the beauty He had designed. He intended her to be at man's side, not behind him or under his feet. Moreover, He intended man to be his woman's "mission field," a seemingly bold statement that every wife understands. An understanding of the word help meet is critical.

The Hebrew word for help meet means to deliver with military force. It is a word that is always used to describe how God delivers us out of sin. Isn't it awesome to know that God did not create women to simply meet the house-help needs of men, but empowered us to deliver our men out of loneliness and lots of other such things?
—Dr. Hyveth Williams
Senior Pastor
Campus Hill Church
Loma Linda, California

However, the world has interpreted the priestly role which God has given to man in his home as Divine direction for the subjugating of all women to all men, thus marginalizing and undermining the true role of womanhood. This structural subjugation of women is pervasive in the Church, which has utilized titles, such as "Father," "Reverend," and a division of labour that assigns menial tasks and roles to women. It is both a reflection and a support system of the worldly patterns of society.

On the contrary, Jesus' ministry, characterized by order and humility, exhibited none of the inequalities that emerged and persist today. However, there is evidence of attempts to ignore and keep women away from Jesus, and to deny them His blessings, in the same way that attempts were made to keep children away from Him. Yet there are several illustrations of the lengths to which women went to break through these imposed structures, and the ways in which Jesus acknowledged and rewarded their break-through efforts. On several occasions He initiated opportunities for women to gain access to Him. Break-through women I called them, a term borrowed from Pastor Lucille Baird of Barbados, W.I. They were simple women, restricted by social and cultural traditions that subjected them to second-class citizenship and attempted to deny them proximity to Jesus and the benefits of His healing and ministry. But Jesus plucked them from obscurity and used their boldness, courage and determination to demonstrate and reward their great faith and show His love and concern for all. More importantly, He lifted them up as examples of the way in which He expects us to live and to love. It is for this reason that He transformed the widow's mite into unbelievable might.

She was widowed and poor, not unlike most of the world's women who are unequally burdened by poverty. According to United Nations statistics, 60 percent of the world's one billion poorest people are women and girls. Two-thirds of the world's 876 million illiterates are female. The statistics continue to drive fear in any but the most callous and uncaring: "Women represent a growing proportion of people living with HIV/AIDS, and in countries with high HIV prevalence, young women and girls with little or no education are at much higher risk than men. Over one-quarter of all women have suffered one form or another of physical abuse, and 80 percent of the victims of armed conflicts are women and children."[11]

Today's world of poor women can indeed identify with the poor widow in Biblical times. Her clothing probably exhibited her financial struggles, nowhere near the fashionable threads that the wealthy and elite wore to the synagogue. She would have had to have walked through the sneers, stares and snobs of the rich to get to the front of the temple to give her offering, not unlike the manner in which a a growing number of churches accept tithes and offerings today.

The rich and powerful must have strutted with well-heeled confidence and self-assurance. They must have dramatically pushed back the flowing sleeves of their elegantly embroidered robes, made of the finest silk and purest linen, in order to proudly deposit their weighty sacks of gold and silver. They did it with "flourish," notes the Clear Word Version (**Mark 12:41**). There must have been a heavy thump that confirmed their value as the sack hit the offering box. I could imagine the widow, head bowed, peeping through the hole in her worn cotton veil, biting her lips as her hand caressed the two coins she had so carefully saved for her offering. She refused to think of the flour or the oil or the piece of fish that they could surely have bought. Perhaps she could have used them to pay for the goods she had received on credit the week before. Two farthings, equivalent to no more than two pennies. But it was all she had. And with as much courage as faith, she was going to give with a merry heart. She hoped no one had seen her. She was glad she had remembered to tie the two coins in the tiny piece of soiled cloth she had found, so that the deposit would be silent and not attract attention. There! She sighed heavily. It was done. No one had observed her.

But Jesus had. He was sitting right next to the offering box, greatly amazed at the wealthy and their tasteless exhibition of grandeur and excess. He may have nodded in recognition of her spirit, but her eyes were on the floor of the temple, her mind focused on her purpose, blocking out even her shame. She knew He was there; but she didn't know that He had seen her. He knew the barriers that she had broken through to accomplish this purpose, so He pointed her out to the disciples, juxtaposing her puny offering and gesture of humility against the ostentatiousness of the rich. In fact, He gathered them together in a huddle and directed their attention to a higher dimension of sacrificial giving:

> *Verily I say unto you, that this poor widow hath cast more in than all they which have cast into the treasury. For all they did cast in of their abundance; but she of her want did cast in all that she had, even all her living.*
> *(Mark 12:43-44)*

According to Pastor Baird: "Jesus took time to teach the disciples the importance of what she gave. He used her as a ministry, the ministry of giving. He used her as a yardstick to define the ministry of giving." Jesus was aware of the break-through efforts of the widow, and He admired, appreciated, and acknowledged her great faith, courage and determination, as He did with so many other women during His ministry.

Similarly, the woman with the issue of blood caught His eye, gained His attention and a healing blessing, all because she broke through the rules and reached out to touch Him. Hers was a break-through from a long, sordid and particularly embarrassing history. Twelve years of suffering from a rare disease that caused her to bleed constantly...the mother of all menstrual flows. It was more than a physical discomfort and restriction. Adherence to cultural traditions that isolated menstruating women kept her in permanent seclusion. Because of her disease, depression, embarrassment, gossip and loneliness became her closest acquaintances. Self-disgust that switched into self-pity were her everyday companions. Frustrated with the helplessness of the many physicians she had visited, she bore her sentence silently...until she heard about Jesus. A ray of hope stirred in her innermost being and began to grow into a holy boldness. The dream of being healed overturned the fear of doing the unthinkable and approaching this Man that was rumoured to be a healer. The possibility of leading a normal life surpassed the anxiety of navigating the crowds that she heard were following Him. And she was right. He was swallowed by crowds of people. In the front-line of this human wall was a group of women, many of whom He had healed and freed from demons: There was Mary Magdalene. He had freed her from not one, but seven demons. Her gratitude was beyond measure, and she was not about to leave Him. In fact, she stayed until the very end, and remained for the new beginning. There was Joanna, the wife of one of Herod's court officials, in regal splendour, and Susanna, dressed in all her finery, as were many of the other women

> *...who used their resources to help Jesus and His disciples*
> *(Luke 8:3 CWV)*

Yes! Many of the women who followed Jesus were not mere hangers-on or knock-abouts. They were financially independent women who used their resources to support His ministry. They were putting their money where their hearts were. I have often wondered why this fact is such a carefully guarded secret, as opposed, for example, to the wiles of Jezebel, Delilah, Potiphar's wife and the other devilish divas.

The woman with the issue of blood indeed may not have been materially wealthy, but she was on a break-through mission; and hence she conquered her fears and joined the throngs following Jesus. She ignored the flash of panic when she saw the crowd of people and realized the impossibility of the task she had set for herself. "I can do this," she whispered to herself. Perhaps she may have been encouraged by the group of women so close to Him. All we know is that she was drawn closer, the crowd pushing her farther one moment, then shoving her closer as they rushed towards Him. But as soon as she was shoved towards Him, she lost her footing and fell to the ground. Her hopes were almost dashed, but she had reached too far to turn back. Then, as if in reward for her determination to continue to press forward, she saw His sandal-shod feet. Somehow, she recognized them from the other feet around her. There was a Divine strength and glow that shone around them and reached out to connect with her and boost her resolve.

With a new burst of enthusiasm, on hands and knees, she crawled through the forest of feet. For a moment it felt as though, instead of being healed, she would be crushed to instant death. Then she caught a glimpse of that Divine foot again, closer this time; close enough that she could stretch her hand to touch. In her innermost being, she knew that even a slight touch would be enough. She closed her eyes tight, stretched her hand toward His Foot, strained against the moving forest, and grabbed. But instead of her determined effort to get at least a touch of His Foot, her hand slightly brushed the hem of His robe. Zap! A bolt of electricity shot through her body, leaving her hot and trembling. She knew she was healed; no question about it. She could feel her own personal Red Sea dry up inside her. But just as she rose to get up to make sure that she was not dreaming, she heard a soft, firm voice that could only be His Voice: "Who touched me?" A momentary relief came with the disciples' near derision of His question in the midst of the multitude. "Master, everyone is pushing and shoving to get close to you. How can you ask, 'Who touched me?'" (*Luke 8:45. CWV*)

But He insisted:

> *Somebody touched me to be healed. I felt power go out from me.* (Luke 8:46 CWV)

Not only had He felt her touch, He recognized the intention of her touch. Busted, she came forth trembling with fear and the afterglow of her healing and confessed her miracle. Jesus knew who she was, and, more importantly, why she was there. But He drew her out in order to display her faith, her courage, her determination and her break-through reward:

> *Don't be afraid. It was your touch of faith that made you whole. Go in peace, and may the blessing of God be with you.* (Luke 8:48, CWV)

It doesn't get better than that. What a contrast! While there is a pervasive tendency to downplay, sideline and silence women, even in today's Church, Jesus uplifted and displayed this woman as a model of break-through faith and courage. He used her, as He used so many other women, as a beacon of faith, humility and courage in the midst of oppression. How much is the Church, and society by extension, suffering from its failure to acknowledge, validate and fully utilize the contribution of women? We have already noted the concept of "Break-Through Women," which Pastor Lucille Baird has shared with us.

Perhaps it is a special space and place to which women are called, in order to accomplish His Plan and Purpose in their lives and in the lives around them. It may well be the key to that all-important development principle of "sustainable livelihoods," which challenges policy makers and planners actively seeking solutions for poverty eradication, and for global peace and security. It is this understanding that undergirds the statement of United Nations Secretary-General Kofi Annan that the future of the world is in the hands of women.

Still the patriarchy of the contemporary Church continues to ignore, play down and suppress the role and function of women, even though women's presence and participation in the ministry of Jesus live as a testimony to the principles of justice, freedom and equality that He modeled. In fact, Jesus often initiated opportunities to show the need to break through traditions. Perhaps it is an awareness of this empathy and particular sensitivity to their oppressed condition that gave women the boldness to touch Him, as did the woman with the issue of blood, even though it was a serious violation of Jewish traditions.

In another event of comparable drama, Jesus used physical deformity as a metaphor for women's social position. The woman with the infirmity had been bent over and bowed down for 18 years with a severe curvature of the spine. Based on current medical knowledge, she was probably a victim of severe osteoporosis, a condition that is linked to menopause. So Christ, in His awesome wisdom, used a woman with a menstrual flow indicating her relative youth, and a woman whose bent frame intimated the cessation of her menstrual flow, to demonstrate the subjection that haunts all women, young as well as old. In addition, we are told that she was possessed by a demon...the demon of oppression and subjection? Her condition had become such a part of her persona, that she did not even think of approaching Him for healing. She was weighted down not only by the demon and the disease, but by the spirit of tradition that provided a nurturing environment for total physical, spiritual and societal oppression.

Jesus invited her to come to Him. He laid hands on her, rebuked the demon and immediately raised her up, straightened her out, turned her loose, got the demon off her back and re-created her spirit, freeing her from domination and subjugation. How suitable a metaphor for women's liberation. How predictable the reaction of the religious leaders. They were scandalized! How dare He break the traditions and heal on the Sabbath? But Jesus was doing more than healing her spiritually and physically. He was releasing her from the traditions that served to subjugate her and to intensify her oppression. Moreover, He used her to straighten out the religious leaders and hypocrites. He acknowledged her humanity and dignity, elevating her status by referring to her as a "Daughter of Abraham," a term that conveyed privilege and blessing.

> *Shouldn't this woman, who is a daughter of Abraham and whom Satan has controlled for the past eighteen years, be set free from her imprisonment on the Sabbath? By the time He had finished speaking, even those who hated Him were ashamed of their attitude, and soon the whole congregation was praising God for what Jesus had done.* **(Luke 13:16-17, CWV)**

In addition to liberating this woman, Jesus underscored the satanic control of social and religious traditions that encouraged, condoned and institutionalized bigotry and prejudice. It is a powerful lesson for social, political and religious leaders who continue to uphold male-dominated societies that oppress women and discriminate against them in flagrant violation of fundamental human rights. Later, as if to drive in his point about the inclusion of women, Jesus used female as well as male references to describe the kingdom of God, comparing it first to male agricultural tasks (*Luke 13:19*), and then to women's household chores.

> *It's like yeast which women use when they bake bread. They mix it in with the dough and the whole batch quietly rises and is soon ready for baking.*
>
> *(Luke 13:21, CWV)*

Jesus continued to exhibit his particular compassion for women when He interjected Himself into the life of the woman who was burying her son. He was her only son; her only child. She had been previously widowed, and her son was her only consolation in a world that was harsh to women, particularly women without male protection. Gone now was not only her source of companionship, but a provider and security in her old age. She could hardly contain her grief, as she wept and wailed, supported by relatives, friends and compassionate neighbours. Always on time, Jesus, on His way to Nain with His own following, met the funeral and stopped respectfully to allow the procession to pass. His glance fell on the grieving woman, and He was overcome with empathy and compassion. The all-knowing, all-caring Jesus knew and felt the pain in her heart. Quietly and without fanfare, He stepped into the funeral. She saw His shadow first, and looked up. Her eyes met His, and instantly a flood of peace and calm engulfed her. "Don't cry," He said gently. And then, quietly, without ceremony, without being asked, He walked toward the open coffin, touched the dead corpse and said:

> *Young man, I am telling you to get up! (Luke 7:14, CWV)*

To the amazement of the crowd, the young man sat up and started to speak. Jesus Himself presented him to his

Mother, who was beside herself with joy. It is clear that Jesus took great pleasure in seeing her mourning turn into dancing, such was His deep understanding and compassion of the woman's circumstances. At the same time, His public concern and caring served notice to His followers of the high esteem with which He held women.

There are more instances in which Jesus went out of His way to eliminate pain and suffering from the lives of women, and to publicly display a deep understanding, caring and sensitivity to their social and economic circumstances. In one of the most dramatic and spectacular of His public lessons, He used a "scarlet" woman to illustrate the social and criminal injustice to which women are subjected. More significantly, He flagged the hypocrisy of those who set themselves up as self-righteous judges of women.

In the midst of one of His teaching sessions in the temple, the Scribes and Pharisees dragged before Jesus a prostitute, whom they claimed to have caught in the process of committing adultery. Many Biblical scholars believe that the religious leaders had actually set up the woman in order to engage Jesus in a debate that would defeat and embarrass Him. Under Mosaic law, the woman would have to be publicly stoned to death. Hence the situation would present a challenge for Jesus to ignore such a proven sin, or to condone and become directly involved in the horror of the public humiliation and death of the woman by stoning. Notice, however, that there was no attempt to shame her male partner, publicly or privately.

The woman must have been frozen stiff with terror...the terror of the public humiliation, and the slow painful death that was sure to follow. This horrible sentence is still carried out in some countries under Islamic law. In a much publicized case in Northern Nigeria at the time of this writing, a young Muslim woman became pregnant after having been separated from her husband. Even though she claimed that the child was her husband's, she had been accused and convicted of adultery. Preparation for her execution included the digging of a hole in which the woman would be placed after first being beaten. Then on-lookers would pick up, first small stones, then large stones hand picked for the occasion, and pummel her immobile body until the last breath was taken. The judge in that case was ready to throw the first stone. Fortunately, international pressure was brought to bear on the case, and the woman was freed. In yet another case in Northern Nigeria, Amina Lawal, a 30-year old mother, lost her appeal against being stoned to death for adultery in an Islamic *sharia* court. If her appeal to a higher court is unsuccessful, she will be publicly stoned to death as soon as she weans her 9-month old daughter. The torture, terror and sheer barbarism of these cases shocked the modern world into global protest for reform and women's human rights.

Today's torture is no different than the torture of the woman accused of adultery in Biblical times. Deeply embarrassed, the woman must have pulled tightly around her the sheet that she had scrambled to cover her naked body. She must have covered her head with it, trying to hide her face, if not her shame. A thousand snapshots of her life must have flashed before her. She must have reflected on the hardships and unfortunate circumstances that had forced her to resort to this shameful profession. She must have been appalled at the hypocrisy of these so-called religious leaders, who had manoeuvred this grand set-up for their own self-righteous purposes. One of those very men might have been the "client" with whom she had been caught in *flagrante delicto*. She must have cringed as she considered the slow, painful and shameful death. She waited for His response, for her sentencing, probably even bracing herself for the first stone. Silence. Then more voices questioning Him, challenging Him,

36

confronting Him, demanding that He make a decision on the punishment that fit this shameful crime. She peeped from behind the dirty bed sheet. Then His voice boomed forth. She was startled, more by the quality of the tone than the volume. There was a double layering of sternness and gentleness, carrying none of the accusation that she had anticipated. In fact, He was not even addressing her.

Any one of you who has never sinned, let him throw the first stone. *(John 8:7, CWV)*

She sighed quietly. What manner of man is this, She thought? Once more she covered her head with the bed sheet, hugging her shivering body tightly as she braced for the first stone. Silence. Fearfully, every so slightly, she dropped the sheet from over her eyes, first because of the silence, then because of the strange grating noise on the floor, as though someone was scraping on the sand. Surely she was hallucinating. Perhaps she was dead already! He was stooping, writing with a stick on the ground. The other religious leaders were watching intently, as though in shock. But the smug look on their faces had been replaced by one of shame and...was that fear? She dropped the sheet a bit lower so she could get a closer look at their faces. Yes, they had paled, and their eyes were full-moon wide. Some even had their mouths opened, an ungainly posture for the proud, self-assured clergy. And then, surely her eyes were failing her, they began to leave. First one, then the other, slowly but surely, the last few scurrying out of the temple, their robes hissing noisily as they fled. She uncovered her head and mustered up the nerve to look at what He was writing on the ground. There, in bold letters, were names...names of all the religious leaders, and there were sins besides these names. Only she was close enough to see. He rose from the ground and she shifted her eyes upwards to see His Face. Was she seeing clearly? Was she mistaken? Was there a twinkle, ever so slight, in His magnificent eyes? She was still trembling with fear, but she couldn't take her eyes away from Him. He kept on looking at her in a half-stern, half-amused, half-pitiful sort of way. She even thought there was an imperceptible wink, and then came that Divine boom of a voice again.

> *Where are all those who were accusing you? It looks like they've gone. There's no one here to condemn you.*
> *(John 8:10, CWV)*

Emboldened by His gentleness, the woman looked around. All of her accusers had fled the temple. "You're right, Lord. There's not a one." Jesus must have smiled at her obvious relief.

> *Neither am I going to condemn you. You're forgiven. You may go now, but leave your life of sin. (John 8:11. CWV)*

Then, to the remaining crowd, and the woman who was leaving slowly, still in shock, He said:

> *I am the light of the world, and the person who follows me will no longer have to feel his way through the darkness, but will be able to walk into the future with certainty because he is following the light.*
> *(John 8:12, CWV)*

Jesus had taken an adulterous woman, elevated her condition to one that served as an object lesson to her accusers, and then freed her from a life of sin and iniquity to walk in His light. Alleluia! Moreover, His stunning response to the accusers of a hapless adulteress was a commentary on tradition, hypocrisy and arrogance and the way in which they interlinked to strangle and subjugate women. There is, too, an unmistakable ripple effect of this triumvirate of tradition, hypocrisy and arrogance. It has wormed its path of evil into the household to support the victimization of women and children, and extended itself into society to support the across-the board discrimination and impoverishment of women. In institutionalized religion, women's roles have been largely decorative and peripheral, in spite of the fact that they comprise the majority of most congregations. To a large extent, male-dominated society has engineered cultural and religious traditions to thwart women's participation, to the detriment of both the Church and society. Liberty and equality were the central focus of Paul's admonition to the churches throughout Galatia.

> *For ye are all the children of God by faith in Christ Jesus. For as many of you as have been baptized into Christ have put on Christ. There is neither Jew nor Greek, there is neither bond nor free, there is neither male nor female: for ye are all one in Christ Jesus. And if ye be Christ's, then are ye Abraham's seed, and heirs according to the promise.* (Gal. 3:26-29, KJV)

In plain, understandable English, we are told:

> *You are grown-up sons and daughters of God through your faith-union with the Lord Jesus Christ. Whoever was baptized in the name of Jesus Christ publicly accepted the life of Christ as a substitute for his own life. No longer is there any spiritual difference between Jews and Gentiles, slaves and free, or males and females. All of us are on the same spiritual level because of our union with Christ. Now if you belong to Christ, then you're a descendant of Abraham and you're entitled to everything that God promised him.* (Gal. 3:26-29, CWV)

This text indeed supports a break-through for women, even though it is hidden in masculinist doctrines that prefer to ignore this important scripture. Yet, there are several break-through directions early in the Bible, that specifically relate to the intended role and function of women. Pastor Baird agrees that the Galatians Scripture is a break through Scripture, but re-emphasizes that the break through for women is contained early in the Old Testament.

> And women have to wait til they reach that? Nah. I broke through in Genesis: 'Let **them** have dominion. Let them have dominion.' And I broke through from there. I'm sorry, I took off like a horse down the road, and I didn't look back. I broke through from the time I read that, I just held my Bible and said, hey! There's no holding me back, because: 'Then God said: ' let us make man in our image'." When He said *man*, He was talking about the male and female species. "According to our likeness. Let *them*, "so He's specific now in what He's saying when He said man, Let *them* (*male* and *female*) have dominion. He didn't say let *him*. Let *them* (two together) have dominion over the fish of the sea, over the birds of the air, over the cattle, over all the earth. And over every creeping thing that creeps on the earth. Let *them*. So I have *dominion*. It's been given to me by God in Genesis 1:26. So I broke through from then. I didn't wait til the New Testament, when he said "and male and female." I didn't wait for that. I broke through years ago, way back up there. And if women can grab that and break through right from the beginning, they got it! They got it made. But unfortunately, they've been socialized in a lot of cultures and so, the way in which they've been indoctrinated has kept them back from seeing that, and men have kept that from them too.
> —Pastor Lucille Baird
> Mt. Zion Ministries
> Barbados, W.I.

But the Bible is replete with women with breakthrough characteristics who were a critical part of His ministry, and who braved great personal danger to stay at the end when the men ran away. The women at the foot of Jesus' cross, and at the mouth of the empty grave have been clothed with the Resurrection power to aid their breakthrough from deception and male subjugation. It is the same power which men have received to overcome societal traditions that condone, encourage and support gender inequality and inequity and to promote justice for all. Such was the bond between Jesus and the women of His ministry. But the roles of these women have largely been buried and undermined by masculinist interpretations, emphases, biases and gender-neutral accounts that cloud women's participation. Yet the early direction in Genesis remains a guiding point that is worth repeating:

> *And God said, Let us make man in our image, after our likeness; and let them have dominion over the fish of the sea, and over the fowl of the air, and over the cattle, and over all the earth, and over every creeping thing that creepeth upon the earth. So God created man in His own image, in the image of God created He him; male and female created He them. And God blessed them, and God said unto them, Be fruitful, and multiply, and replenish the earth, and subdue it: and have dominion over the fish of the sea, and over the fowl of the air, and over every living thing that moveth upon the earth.*
>
> *(Gen. 1:26-28, KJV)*

Genderstanding Jesus:
Questions for Reflection, Discussion and Action
Chapter 3

1). Do you think that the structural subjugation of women in the society is reflected and supported in the Church?

2). Do you think that the Church encourages the participation of women at leadership levels?

3). How much is the Church, and society by extension, suffering from its failure to acknowledge, validate and fully utilize the contribution of women?

4). Do you believe that the future of the world is in the hands of women?

5). How can the Church become a more enabling force in the lives of women?

6). Are you confronted—individually or collectively—with a situation that needs break-through faith?

Chapter 4

THOSE NO-TURNING BACK WOMEN

Stubbornness in women is a quality that is frequently undervalued, not usually equated with femininity, and often perceived as intimidating to men. This same quality that is applauded as male persistence and determination becomes a negative in women. Whenever I am accused of being stubborn, I am sure to point out that stubbornness is a quality more accurately applied to children. Strong women make informed choices and follow through, even if it goes against popular opinions. There are many representations in the Bible of women who displayed stubbornness of purpose to break through barriers, hurdle strong obstacles and overcome attempts to keep them from experiencing the grace of Jesus, simply because they possessed a strong determination and self-direction. There were many attempts to restrict women who sought to minister to Jesus, not unlike the way in which women are restricted from participating in contemporary Christianity. In one particular case, Jesus set up the scene Himself, in order to teach His disciples a most important lesson—that of egalitarianism under God.

In the case of the Syrophoenician woman, whose gender and ethnicity made communication with a Jewish male politically and culturally incorrect, Jesus laid out His own egalitarian position and challenged the discriminatory power of traditions. He placed Himself in the way of this distraught mother, with the specific intention of making His case to His disciples. At first He ignored her cries for the healing of her demon-possessed daughter. This action was totally in tune with discriminatory and prejudicial practices against non-Jews, and the disciples offered to get rid of the bothersome woman (Matthew 15:23). Indeed, it had taken all of the woman's courage and determination to defy cultural practices to approach the Jewish healer. Probably she had heard of His particular compassion towards women. It was possible too that she had heard of His fairness and justice that challenged hierarchical and discriminatory customs and practices. Or, she may have simply been tired of the life of alienation and suspicion to which anyone possessed with the devil was subjected. She could no longer bear the suffering of her daughter.

Using desperation as motivation, she mustered up all the persistence and determination she had, and headed to the coastal region of Tyre and Sidon, where she heard He had been performing healing miracles. When she first laid eyes on Him, her reality almost conquered her resolve. 'How dare she approach this Man, whom many believed was the Son of God? At the very least He was a Jewish Rabbi, and completely out of her sphere of contact. But the thought of her suffering child spurred her on. Abruptly, as if pushed by some internal force, she jumped in front of Him:

> *Have mercy on me, Lord, son of David. My daughter is possessed by a devil.* (Matthew 15:22, CWV)

Jesus stopped and regarded her with a stare that pierced her every nerve and sinew. At first she was surprised by His response that His commitment was to help the Israelites—not her ethnic group—but she had come too far to turn back. Moreover, He was her daughter's last hope. Her daughter's suffering, her own pain and the shame and disgrace to which the family had been subjected propelled her argument in the face of His rebuff. She had come for

His healing and His blessing, and she was not about to let attention to cultural norms stand in her way. Moreover, if He were indeed the Lord and Saviour that rumours said He was, she knew that He would not, no, could not bow to mere traditions of man. She was going to give it another shot of stubborn persistence. She bowed low, and again begged Jesus for the healing miracle of which she knew He was capable. But this God/Man knew her spirit, and was bent on using her as His object lesson.

> *It's not right to take the family dinner and give it to the dogs.* **(Matthew 15:26 CWV)**

Ouch! He called her a dog! She could hardly believe her ears. How the disciples and others in close hearing-range must have been scandalized! He sounded like they did. It served this little pushy, low-class, Gentile woman right, but surely this harsh response was out of character for Him. Little did they know that Jesus was intentionally giving them a taste of their own medicine, shocking them by repeating the very words they used to Gentiles, modeling the lack of compassion and humanity they showed to those they thought were beneath them. But, as Jesus well knew, this no-turning-back woman was not about to be turned around. The vision of her demon-filled daughter danced before her eyes, but she did not blink. She could almost hear the demon laughing vilely. And in one of those rare moments in Jesus' ministry, she went toe to toe with Him. She challenged Him, relying firmly on the rumours of His goodness and His kindness, and the gentleness she saw and felt in His Presence. "That's true, Lord," she agreed diplomatically, "but family dogs are taken care of by their owners and are given the leftovers." (Matthew 15:27, CWV).

The disciples were stunned. What cheek! She was calling out Jesus. "Put your money where your mouth is!"

she might have well said. Surely this great Lord and Saviour was big enough to break-through established customs to meet the need of the oppressed. He was big enough to flout religious prescriptions that were more concerned about legalisms and rituals than ministering to human pain and suffering. After all, this was the same Jesus who argued against Pharisaic beliefs that tried to prevent Him from healing on the Sabbath Day. Certainly He could connect the dots and break-through similar traditions and prejudices that would prevent the healing of her daughter. She was not going to allow Him to use culture to turn her around. Moreover, if all He could offer her were crumbs or left-overs, she had enough faith and confidence in Him to know that was more than enough to provide the necessary healing of her daughter. She was an aggressive and unrepentant crumb snatcher.[12] I imagine that Jesus smiled and thought: "You go, girl" But instead, in a loud, compassionate and authoritative voice that carried the message intended for the disciples, He responded:

> *Dear woman, you have a very strong faith. I really do care about you and your daughter. Your request is granted and your daughter is now well.*
> *(Matthew 15:28, CWV)*

And, according to one Biblical interpretation:

> *The disciples then realized that Jesus was revealing the contrast between their cold cultural bias and the compassion that God wanted them to have.*
> *(Matthew 15:28, CWV)*

---

12   I thank Assistant Pastor Trevor Kinlock of Emmanuel Seventh-day Adventist Church of Brinklow, Maryland, for this appropriate terminology of "crumb snatcher."

Jesus not only permitted this woman to communicate with Him, He baited her into a debate and discussion that demonstrated her strong faith and stubborn determination in the midst of overwhelming odds. He had placed Himself in her way, with the specific intention of making His case to His disciples, aware of their own prejudices and bigoted views. In a manner similar to the way in which He had used the woman caught in adultery as a public example of the tyranny of tradition and the hypocrisy and arrogance that often accompanied it, He used this Syrophoenician woman, not only to defy tradition, but to show the depth of faith of many who are outside of the closed circle of the so-called chosen. So many are called; how few will be chosen? Moreover, here is a graphic illustration of the dignity and humanity of each person in God's eyes, regardless of gender, race, ethnicity, creed, culture or age. Indeed this exhibited His approval, admiration and solidarity with women's struggle for equality and justice. It was a solidarity that women recognized, appreciated and acknowledged.

Pastor Brenda Billingy sees this incident as a role-playing strategy used by Jesus to give the disciples a close-up view of their own prejudiced notions, knowing full well that the woman possessed a faith mature enough to maximize the effect of His demonstration.

> I love the story of the Syrophoenician woman. It used to bother me that He called her a dog. But it shows sometimes that our English language doesn't really give fair expression to what was going on. It wasn't until I looked at the Greek words in that story that I got excited. First they started off with the disciples saying "send her away, she's bothering us." His mind-set was: "You all are not getting it. You're not understanding how we're supposed to treat people, so let me do some reflection here, and see if you can catch it. Role play. I think He was role-playing for them. He starts off by using the words

that they used. Now they frequently would refer to people as dogs if they were not of their class, and particularly the Gentiles were always referred to as dogs. So He starts off by using their language, so that they could see how harsh they respond to people. But, this woman realizes that Jesus is trying to teach them a lesson, so girl-friend jumps in the role-play, and she begins to respond. He calls her the dog first, but she has sense enough to respond with: "Yea, I must be a dog, but…'and when I look at the word she used for dog, it's a '**pet**.' It's a **pet**. And she's saying—and we see it in this country—there are people who will treat their pets better than they will treat people. So she's saying. I know You are not like these men. You're trying to teach them a lesson. They called me a dog, but I know You will treat me as your "pet." Just give me your crumbs from the table, and we're cool. It's master and pet. When I discovered that in scripture, it revolutionized my thought. Because, all of a sudden, I figured you know what, it's the same thing we're dealing with. The men didn't get it. But the woman got it, and she realized who she was dealing with, and she said: "Forget them. I'm dealing with you. I don't care what they call me. I don't care how they refer to my background, it doesn't make a difference. I'm dealing with you, and I know you're different; I know you're not going to treat me the way they treat me. So even if you say crumbs, I know it's going to be a good thing, because it's totally different from what they're talking about.

—Pastor Brenda Billingy
Bladensburg Seventh-day Adventist Church
Maryland

The recognition of the need to have a direct relationship with Jesus Christ, to decipher role play from reality, and to listen and accurately interpret His directives are critical lessons for women and men alike. More often than not, it is the difference between succumbing to man-made restrictions and being elevated through Divine directions.

The other word I looked up was crumbs. It's not when you eat all your food and there's a little bit left. It referred me to the crumbs of the feeding of the five thousand. So when I looked that up, it said it was not just scraps that people had eaten and left. He had divided the bread, just like you would take a loaf of bread and cut it up. And then what was not used, was considered the crumbs. So girlfriend said: "I know your **'crumbs'** is more than enough. Give me **crumbs**. I don't care what they call it. Give me **crumbs**. That's more than enough for me." And so, it's all about knowing who you're dealing with; what God is able to provide; His willingness to deal with you. And when Jesus realized that she caught it, when He realized that she understood what was going on in that little dialogue, He said, "your faith is a little bit much. You got it!" And this was not a Christian, per se, in their eyesight, but she had faith enough to understand who she was dealing with, and she was willing to seek Him out and to receive whatever He had to give to her. It's the same concept we're dealing with in these days. When the men don't get it, God will deal with the women, regardless of who they are, as long as they are willing to take and do whatever He says, regardless of what people call you, regardless of whether they think you should be there or not, He's saying: It's me and you. Doesn't have anything to do with these guys. I am teaching them a lesson on the side, but you and I must be on the same level.

—Pastor Brenda Billingy
Bladensburg Seventh-day Adventist Church
Maryland

Couched in this story of Jesus' encounter with the Syrophoenician woman are specific directions for women about their relationship to God, and their focus on His Purpose and His Intent. He says "crumbs," we accept crumbs with its innate limitations, but His intention and translation may well be the richest, most filling meal. The question remains: are we settling for a meager meal, while missing the fabulous feast that has been prepared? Are we getting up from the table still hungry, while leaving a sumptuous meal untouched? Even more worrying, because we have been socialized to be satisfied with the crumbs we are thrown, are we neglecting to invite others to partake in this sumptuous meal, unaware of the lavish leftovers that are meant to be widely shared?

It is a story that emphasises the Divine connection, an ability to breakthrough traditional social, political and religious structures to make and maintain a Divine relationship. Through this Divine relationship, the direction for women in His Ministry comes. Obedience becomes key, surmounting traditions to find, cling to and stubbornly follow that path to which we've been directed. While it is a continuing struggle for all Christians, it becomes an even greater challenge for Christian women, and an imperative for women called to the Ministry.

> For women in Ministry, you gotta get to that point. Must get to that point. So I particularly appreciate those references. Even though they are not widespread in Scripture, I think the Lord allowed enough to be included, and not just included from the standpoint of naming them, but the standpoint of His recognition of what they had done, and His public appreciation for what they had done.
>
> —Pastor Brenda Billingy
> Bladensburg Seventh-day Adventist Church
> Maryland

One of the most dramatic examples of women's appreciation of Jesus' support and kindness to them is revealed in the story of the woman with the alabaster box. The debate still rages as to whether this woman was a prostitute, whether she was a woman of means who had lived a sinful life, or whether she was Mary Magdalene. It is within this context that the mystery around Mary Magdalene continues. Was she a woman of easy virtue? Was she the adulterer who Jesus Christ saved from a vicious death by stoning? Or, was she an independently wealthy woman, who, having received forgiveness from Jesus, continued to support His ministry? Was she the same Mary of Bethany, sister of Martha and Lazarus, and dear friend of Jesus? (John 12) These questions, and the various interpretations which they inspire, highlight some of the critical issues that surround accepted representations of women in the Bible.

The woman with the alabaster box, for example, is noted as "a woman in the city, which was a sinner"(*Luke 7:37, KJV*). This is updated to "a woman who had lived a sinful life in that town" (*NKJV*). However, the notes for this verse describe her as "a prostitute." In the *CWV*, she is labeled outright as "a prostitute from town". Through *genderstanding* lenses, there appears to be a broad leap from a woman who leads a sinful life, to a woman who is a prostitute. This decidedly urbane woman may very well have been living with a man who was not her husband, as did the Samaritan woman whom Jesus met at the well. That situation would indeed have made her an object of town gossip, and her sin public. But, a prostitute? If indeed she was Mary Magdalene, named as one of the women "who used their resources to help Jesus and His disciples." (*Luke 8:3. CWV*), she may have been independently wealthy, which would have given her greater visibility and notoriety, not to mention envy. It is ironic how easily descriptions of public sin, and wealth become "prostitution" for a woman. Indeed it points to the ease with which our thought patterns are directed through male-dominated mind-sets that immediately ascribe the worst interpretations to women, especially when there is a hint of any form of independence. Would an immediate link be made between a man who is a wealthy, public sinner to prostitution?

It is clear, however, that this woman was an uninvited guest. This was the home of Simon, a wealthy man. Some Biblical scholars intimate that Simon himself had been the person with whom she had been leading a life of sin, which would certainly have made his home off-limits to her. Indeed, he was in utter shock at seeing her at his fancy dinner party. Others claim that Simon was her uncle; and still others argue he was her brother-in-law, husband of her sister, Martha. Either of these scenarios implies a sexual link that screams incest, making Jesus' later admonition to Simon even more powerful and instructive. We know for sure, however, that she was a woman named Mary, a point to be revisited in a subsequent chapter.

The party had been the talk of the town, and only the rich and powerful, the *creme de la creme* of society, had been invited. Simon, as host, could not believe that she had managed to slip by his security guards, who had been given specific instructions to allow only those with the cherished invitations to enter. Not only had she crashed the party, she seemed determined to accomplish some mission. It was a two-fold mission. First, she wanted to express thanks or seek healing for her sinful condition, depending on the specific persona applied to this woman. One reading of Jesus' comments to Simon, the host, implies that the woman had previously met and received spiritual healing from Jesus. Secondly, she was saddened by the constant news and references from His own mouth of His impending death, and had come to minister to Jesus before His Crucifixion. It was an event to which Jesus frequently referred, but which His male disciples consistently failed to acknowledge or internalize. They just didn't get it! Women, precisely because of their structural subordination and oppression, were good listeners. Our very lives depend on it. They listened. They read between the lines. They connected the dots. She got it!

Hers was a bold move; but, encouraged by the pervasive rumours of the way in which Jesus Himself touched
women, His gentleness and particularly His kindness
toward women, she pressed on, not turning back. Surely it
must have been this knowledge of His particular sensitivity to women and their oppressed circumstances that
propelled this daring act. She could feel the nasty stares on
her back as she entered; Simon's accusatory glare was
palpable. "What was she, a public sinner doing in the
presence of these august city notables?" he thought
audibly. She trembled, shivered in her sandals, even
tripped once, but she was not turning back. She did not
even dare look at Him. Full of humility and gratitude, she
concentrated on His feet.

> *She came to where Jesus was reclining like the other
> guests, with His feet away from the table. She knelt
> down, kissed His feet and wet them with her tears. She
> then dried them with her hair, opened the little jar and
> poured the expensive perfume on His feet.*
> *(Luke 7:38, CWV)*

Many saw, and stopped eating to watch. Others were
too busy talking and eating to see this spectacular demonstration of love and gratitude in action. But when she
opened the tiny jar of rare spices and its delightful
fragrance cut through the air, everyone came to attention.
She had gone too far to turn back now, so she stayed the
course and concentrated on her purpose—a lesson for all
women. As she poured the ointment and began to massage
His aching feet, the fragrance of lavender wafted through
the air, its sweetness commanding the attention and
commentary of all the guests. Simon was beside himself
with anger, but he remained immobilized by the sheer
boldness of the act, still unable to grasp its deep significance: anointment for His burial and Resurrection and his,

Simon's, and our Salvation. Although Simon said not a word, Jesus read his thoughts…thoughts that challenged His Divinity: "How can this man be a prophet, much less the Messiah? If He were what He claims to be, He would know that she's a prostitute and wouldn't let her near Him." (*Luke 7:39, CWV*)

Even though Jesus was intent on teaching the arrogant, sinful Simon a lesson, He was well-mannered enough not to embarrass his host. He quietly told him the story comparing the two debtors, one owing considerably more than the other. When Simon agreed that the person with the larger debt would indeed be more grateful for forgiveness, Jesus, again in *soto voce*, compared the careless reception He had received from Simon, to the extravagant show of humility, gratitude and appreciation by the woman. Jesus began a stunning comparison between the Mighty Simon and the woman at His feet; between the powerful and the powerless; the prideful and the thankful; the arrogant and the compassionate. Using the woman at His feet as an illustration of God's limitless forgiving love versus Pharisaical arrogance and hypocrisy, He said:

> *Though people call her a prostitute, she asked me to forgive her and I did.*   (Luke 7:47, CWV)

Surely Jesus would have admonished those who today continue to refer to this woman as a prostitute. While Jesus' words may have touched Simon's pride-full heart, Judas could not contain himself. Driven by greed, deception and an insatiable hunger for power, he grumbled about the waste of the cost of the expensive fragrance that could have been sold and given to him, in "safe" keeping for the poor. More than anyone else, Judas didn't get it! Couldn't get it, so preoccupied was he with his own worldly concerns of wealth, power and material gain. Some writers go further to infer that Judas' grumbling

went beyond concern for extravagant spending to asper-
sions of underlying sexual attentions that the woman may
have had towards Jesus. Here we see unmasked the
undeniable difficulty of men to move beyond narrow,
bigoted views of women as sexual objects to an appreciation of their real substance, value and potential. It is an
erroneous perception that lingers today and continues to
influence decisions about the leadership roles of women in
the church, particularly with respect to ordination in most
denominations. We are told that the men gossiped about
her. It is no accident, then, that Jesus, with Divine
omniscience, proclaimed universal and timeless memori-
alizing of this one act of love and gratitude of this no
turning-back woman.

> *I tell you that wherever the gospel is preached around
> the world, her act of kindness and love will also be
> preached as a memorial to her.*   *(Mark 14:9, CWV)*

It is noteworthy that Mark is the only disciple who saw
this prediction important enough to commit to writing. It
is this disobedience of Jesus' implied command of
widespread preaching of the word of the woman with the
alabaster box that has continued to marginalise women's
contributions. Moreover, it is the failure to follow the
model of His Divine inclusion and illustration through His
strategic employment of women in His Ministry that has
left room for satan's brilliant strategy of gender division. It
is a strategy that continues to thwart the spread of the
gospel. Indeed, a double whammy! Instead, and more
critically, preference has been given to texts that record
cultural traditions that discriminate against women.
What's more, these texts have been pulled out of context to
discourage and minimize women's contribution through
diverse ways of condemning them to "silence." This in
spite of the powerful command to all to "Go, Tell." Hence

Jesus ensured that the woman with the alabaster box got equal quality time:

> He gave time to listen to her, and to be ministered to by her. He could have pushed her away, because as the disciples said, 'if He was a man of God, surely He would know who was touching Him.' But what He did, He entertained her, 'cause her role to Him was important. She took time to minister to Him, preparing Him for His burial. And guess what? All of those men around Him, they never saw Him coming to His time of burial. Crucifixion. But she saw, and she was used as a vessel to prepare Him for His death. So the women's roles in His Life at that point were very significant, but the disciples, and the apostles as they became and our modern day men play those roles down. It is unfortunate.
>
> —Pastor Lucille Baird
> Mt. Zion Ministries
> Barbados, W.I.

As the story unfolds, Jesus smiled gently with the woman with the alabaster box, and said: *"Thy sins are forgiven."* She dried her tears, relief beginning to show on the tear-stained face. And He said to the woman: *"Thy faith hath saved thee; go in peace."* The woman left in a flood of joy. If indeed she was Mary Magdalene, she did not go far, for we read later of the material and financial support she gave to His ministry. She could not have gone far, because we see her at the foot of the cross. She stayed connected to Him, because we see her in a front-row seat at the open grave on that Resurrection Sunday. Thank God for the <u>Resurrection power</u> that has enabled women to break through the barriers of subjugation and discrimination and to continue to advance in the midst of oppression, repression and strategic exclusion. Thank God for the <u>special grace</u> and <u>strength</u> given to women that enabled them to stay <u>loyal,</u> <u>connected</u> and <u>faithful</u> to Jesus, even when the disciples betrayed, denied and deserted Him.

Some scholars believe that it was that very evening that Judas, angered by the action of the woman and jealous of the high praise Jesus heaped on her, left Simon's house and proceeded directly to the chief priests to betray Jesus. How is the mission of Christ betrayed by a male-dominated Church that continues to subjugate women and limit their roles through man-made constraints that challenge and disobey God's word and attempt to torpedo His mission and Purpose? It is a frightful and dangerous thought, for in contrast to Christ's commendation of the woman with the alabaster box, He says about Judas:

> *I feel sorry for the man who is going to betray me. It would have been better for him if he had never been born than to grow up to do this sort of thing.*
> **(Mark 14:21, CWV)**

Experiences of male domination have not only prevented women's contribution to the spread of the gospel, but have blocked the ears of many who see only the incompatibility of discrimination against women in the Church with the message of Christ's saving grace for all. More critically, in worst case scenarios, the extreme domination of men has reached into households to influence male behavioral patterns that set the stage for domestic violence and incest. In addition, male-dominated societal structures have crafted laws and practices that condone rather than condemn this behaviour. The reluctance with which we see these structures beginning to crumble beneath the pressure of women's activism worldwide—supported by many enlightened and committed men—is evidence of the degree to which they have been entrenched, and become the architect of innate evil. The question remains: which activity do we choose, support and promote by our very action or non-action? Do we choose the woman with the alabaster box; or do we choose Judas and his betrayal?

In stark contrast to the scattered disciples, the women remained at the foot of the cross, pooling their forces and resources to the very end for the new beginning. They refused to be turned back. In spite of the minimized role that contemporary Christianity still ascribes to women, a careful examination of The Word will foreground the significance of women's activities during Jesus' Crucifixion and Resurrection.

> They use the fact that Jesus chose 12 men to be disciples, and then eventually to be apostles as a yardstick to measure how Jesus feels about women, but they have lost track of the fact that He spent a lot of time with women. He spent a lot of time caring for them, and them caring for Him, reciprocating back to Him. Ministry on both sides. He ministered to them, He took time to be with them, and He made pointers about them.
>
> —Pastor Lucille Baird
> Mt. Zion Ministries
> Barbados, W.I.

Indeed it is only through careful *genderstanding* of the Bible that the activities of women in Jesus' Ministry and in the early Church begin to emerge with new significance and meaning. Because the male-dominated Church has either deliberately or unconsciously buried or strategically sidelined them, it is important to excavate women's presence and activities between the lines and to hear their voices betwixt the words. Although the Word of God, the Bible has been subjected to several interpretations and translations, which would have been influenced by masculinist viewpoints and patriarchal traditions. But women played such important roles that it has been impossible to completely exclude or erase them. What man may have excluded, God had included for the same purpose He created Eve…to serve as a fully capable companion, endowed with equal intelligence and perhaps even more compassion. However, the exclusion of women has undermined the teamwork and team spiritedness that was the Divine intention. Man-made strategic exclusion versus Divine inclusion. Jesus was clear in His command that Mary's magnanimous act of worship, adoration and caring should be memorialized all over the world. Has this command been obeyed?

And if not, why not? Nowhere is this Divine inclusion more dramatic, more deliberate, more inescapable than at the climax of Jesus' Ministry at Calvary.

The role and significance of women in Jesus' Death and Resurrection, indeed the supreme *raison d'etre* for His purpose on earth, is indisputable. While it is not a frequent topic of sermons, and it is often mentioned only in passing, the activities and behaviour of the women around Jesus stand out in stark contrast to that of the male disciples. According to one female pastor, if these activities had been attributed to men, they would have been the subject of many more sermons. For women appeared to have grasped the substance of His Mission in a way that the male disciples, in spite of their closeness to Jesus, simply did not. It is difficult to resist comparing the male concern about His earthly powers, and their competition for status in His Kingdom, against the humility of the women. Women's humble attention enabled them to hear and grasp His constant reminders of His impending death and to make the necessary preparations. Early understanding that His earthly days were numbered was demonstrated by the woman with the alabaster box; hence she proceeded to anoint Him in preparation for His burial.

> *She has done what she could and perfumed my body for burial.* **(Mark 14:9, CWV)**

On the contrary, that same afternoon Judas betrayed Him into the hands of his enemies. Not long after, Peter denied Him, not once, but three times, as the remainder of the men scattered like sand in a heavy wind. When, at the moment of His most intense agony, He found a quiet place to pray to His father for the necessary courage and strength that His humanity would require, the disciples fell asleep. The women, on the other hand, vigilant, industrious and prepared with spices for His burial, followed at a distance. But they were there: watching every tiny detail, waiting, weeping and wailing, so that they could give an accurate account. They were the ones who saw Joseph of Aramathea take possession of His Body and lay it in the tomb. Indeed Joseph had some help from other men who were followers, but there is no record of the presence of any of the other disciples, except John.

Some of the women, however, are called by name: Among them were Mary Magdalene, and Mary the Mother of James, the younger and of Joses, and Salome. In Galilee these women had followed him and cared for His needs. Many other women who had come up with Him to Jerusalem were also there. (Mark 15:40-41, NIV)

The women rested on the Sabbath, but on Sunday morning they were ready. Armed with the fragrant spices, they set out to claim His body. There is nothing like a no-turning-back woman bent on accomplishing a mission, and so the sisters moved **early** that Resurrection morning. When they arrived at the tomb as the sun was rising, they realized that, in spite of their honourable intention and their awesome determination, they were lacking the physical strength to get into the tomb. *"Who will roll away the stone from the door of the tomb for us?"* they asked each other (*Mark 16:3, NKJV*). But the deed was already done. Halle-lujah! The stone had been rolled away, and the women were first-hand witnesses to the fulfilling of God's Divine promise and the awesome revelation of His power. Immediateley they carried the news to the disciples. Where were the male disciples? They were hiding in a room, fearful, confused, unprepared, not knowing what to do. What is even more instructive, is that they did not believe the women who had followed the instructions of the angel:

> But go, tell His disciples—and Peter—that He is going before you into Galilee; there you will see Him, as He said to you. (Mark 16:7, NKJV)

According to tradition only the word of two men could be believed. Hence the disciples sent two men to the tomb to confirm the word of the women, allowing man's tradition to supersede God's direction. It is further instructive that Mary Magdalene, whose identity and status continue to be debated later returned to the tomb alone, weeping, and became the first to hear His Voice.

> Woman, why weepest thou? Whom seekest thou? (John 20:15, KJV)

Mary became the first person to whom Jesus spoke after His Resurrection. Thinking the voice belonged to the caretaker of the tomb, she related her fears that someone had stolen the Body of the Lord. Then, Jesus called her name, as only He could.

> Mary! (John 20:16)

Immediately she recognized His voice. "Master, is that you?" (John 20:16, KJV) She ran to the disciples to take the news that He was alive, because she had seen Him, and He had talked to her; called her by name! Moreover, He had given her a message to give to them. (*John 20:17*) Here again is an example of Divine inclusion instead of man's strategic exclusion of women. The women were pro-active because they were Divinely guided, but their inspired involvement was challenged. The disciples did not believe the women, because they were deafened by a jostling for power that had clouded Jesus' constant words to them. Blinded by arrogance and sexism, they could not see the women's loyalty and importance to His ministry. They could not believe the women, because to do so would question their own actions. Consumed by fear, disbelief, and perhaps some measure of jealousy that Jesus would appear first to the women—and even speak to one, the disciples remained in hiding, terrified that the enemies of Jesus would come after them. There they remained, until Jesus walked through the doors of their hiding place to get them and remind them that He was who He said He was; and had done what He said He had come to do. A message that the women had already grasped, internalized and acted upon.

Jesus was aware of those who possessed the true grit in His Ministry. In addition, He would have known that women's leadership roles would be minimized and side-lined in the establishment of His Church. He would have known the censure, ridicule and oppression to which women would be subjected, all under the guise of carrying out His word. Hence He took great pains, throughout His life on earth, and poignantly after His Resurrection, to ensure a place for women. This inclusive stance on behalf of women is violated by male-dominated religious traditions and institutions at the risk of blunting the impact of His work, thwarting its spread and stymying its growth. The negative impact of male domination on society continues to be the most convincing proof of God's intention to fully integrate women and employ their skills and talents in disseminating His Word and executing His Work. In the next chapter, we explore the specific direction Jesus gives about His intended work for women.

Genderstanding Jesus:

Questions for Reflection, Discussion and Action

Chapter 4

1). Do you consider yourself a "No Turning-Back Woman?" Why?

2). Are you settling for a meager meal of "crumbs," while leaving a filling meal untouched?

3). Is the mission of Christ being betrayed by a male-dominated Church that continues to subjugate women and limit their roles through man-made constraints that challenge and disobey God's word and attempt to torpedo His mission and Purpose?

4). Which activity do you choose, support and promote by your very action or non-action: the woman with the alabaster box; or Judas and his betrayal?

5). Jesus was clear in His command that Mary's magnanimous act of worship, adoration and caring was to be memorialized all over the world. Has this command been obeyed? If not, why not?

Chapter 5

OUT OF THE KITCHEN!

Whether we care to admit it or not, there is a connecting thread that runs between the division of labour in the home, religious doctrines that place men at the head of the household and domestic abuse against women and children. Somehow, the religious *dictum* of men as spiritual heads of their homes has been coopted and used to transform women into resident house maids and men into imperial couch potatoes presiding over remote controls that move deftly from sports programme to sports programme. In worst case scenarios, this male-domination that translates into male helplessness, disinterest and near physical retardation in the home robs children of quality involvement with their fathers. At the same time overworked, stressed-out mothers struggle single-handedly to reach impossible superwoman goals.

The preceding chapter details the actions of the women during the Crucifixion and Resurrection of Jesus Christ that demonstrate clearly the unique role they had been destined to play, and the <u>courage</u>, <u>sense of purpose</u>, <u>determination</u>, <u>fearlessness</u> and <u>selflessness</u> that they employed. Could Jesus then have intended women to play a secondary role in a mission that He knew would be challenging, thank-less, dangerous and would require every skill, talent and strategy available to humankind? Moreover, it was a mission that would require <u>service</u>, <u>humility</u> and <u>steadfastness,</u> with a pervasive theme of equality and a heart for the oppressed and down-trodden.

Who more than women—then and now—understand subordination and oppression at the gut level? Through-out Jesus' Ministry, His deliberate attempts to include women at critical junctures carry a message which the contemporary Church seems bent on ignoring and/or reinterpreting to promote male supremacist interests.

It is in this context that some of the most heated debates on women's leadership roles in the Church continue, particularly with respect to women as ordained, full-service preachers and pastors. Arguments that reserve the pulpit strictly for men have been used to confine women to subservient positions, to keep them serving instead of, or in addition to, leading, to keep their visibility and capability confined to the pew and the kitchen. There is, however, an unmistakable clarity in Jesus' position, in another lesson on the danger of adhering to traditions that confined women to subordinate roles.

Picture the incident of the overnight visit of Jesus and His disciples at the home of Martha and Mary. Under normal circumstances, the act of entertaining house or dinner guests is accompanied by some measure of anxiety, even for the most gracious and prepared host or hostess. Could you imagine the panic of entertaining the Saviour? And even though Jesus' humility, thoughtfulness and caring would have made Him an easy guest, one can imagine the self-imposed pressure and special care in having everything to near perfection. Appropriately named, Martha appears to have been the Biblical Martha Stewart. A natural tendency to detail, a heightened sense of the esthetics and her great love and awe of Jesus would have multiplied the self-imposed stress of entertaining Him. Were the serving utensils without spots? Check the water pitcher for cracks. Is the water cool enough? Can't let the bread get cold. Where are the leaves she had carefully picked and cleaned to keep the bread warm? Was He tired of eating fish? Wish she had picked some more grapes from the vineyard. Martha must have been in a state of controlled panic.

In addition, the men must have been tired and hungry, and of course, they were not about to help. One could understand the urge to have the food properly prepared, the rugs in the eating area neatly spread, and the dinner utensils carefully laid out. Martha, too, wanted to be a part of the conversation and to benefit from Jesus' teaching. What a learning experience sitting at Jesus' feet! But it was Mary who was soaking it all up, benefitting from Jesus' teaching, as her sister Martha hustled around the kitchen. When things got a little more than she could handle, and the proverbial water became more than flour, she went to Jesus for help. What a powerful reminder of Jesus' concern about even our most trivial concerns. "Lord don't You care anything about how much work it takes to feed all of these men? The least You can do is tell my sister to help me." (*Luke 10:40, CWV*)

Contrary to popular interpretations, the intention of Jesus' response was not to upbraid the meticulous Martha. In fact, He went out of His way to first commend her thoughtfulness and to applaud her caring and concern for beauty and order.

> *Martha, Martha, thou art careful and troubled about many things.* (Luke 10:41, KJV)

The Clear Word version is even more specific:

> *Martha, Martha, you are helpful to everyone in need and you're going to great length to feed us and make us comfortable.* (Luke 10:41, CWV)

Jesus acknowledged and appreciated her efforts. His warning, however, addressed the need to prioritize the spiritual, undergird the material with the spiritual, and to integrate both to ensure balance. Some scholars read into Jesus' comment an observation of the one-sided preoccupation of women with nurturing others, even at the expense of their own personal and spiritual development. It is a task imposed by a male-dominated society that aggravates the situation by positioning male involvement in domestic tasks as "unmanly." Women themselves often unknowingly collaborate in their own subordination by socializing boys to consider housework as work fit only for girls or "sissies." This understanding of the division of labour is central to the structural subjugation of women, in which so-called "feminine" tasks, while of critical value to the care of humanity and—in more macroeconomic and political terms—the production of labour, are considered of low value socially and financially. This devaluing of women's labour not only subjugates women, but devalues men who attempt to move out of these confined role divisions to be more helpful in the hands-on provision for their families. For example, younger men who are more inclined to greater hands-on involvement with child rearing are seen as going against socially accepted norms for male behaviour. Jesus' next statement to Martha throws cold water on every attempt to keep women confined to roles that are subservient, invisible and purely domestic.

> *But one thing is needful: and Mary hath chosen that good part, which shall not be taken away from her.*
> *(Luke 10:42, KJV)*

Here, with great clarity, Jesus promotes the need for women to be spiritually trained and developed. And in full fore-knowledge of the particular challenge women must face in this area, even in His Name, He warns that Mary must be vigilant and protective of this right of spiritual development and training...*which shall not be taken away from her.* Another translation gets to the core of the problem.

> *But there are more important things than food and comfort. Mary came to me because she recognizes her need. She has done the right thing. The things I'm telling her will help her the rest of her life.* (Luke 10:42, CWV)

This admonition is not to be taken lightly. Jesus' support of Mary's move out of the kitchen, and her desire to prioritize spiritual and intellectual development is a major breakthrough in understanding God's intention for utilizing women's skills and talent. As a female minister and the president of the Pan African Christian Women Alliance (PACWA), an organisation which encourages women to become aware of their own calling, Pastor Annette Taylor of Liberia has encountered opposition by male ministers and other men in the Body of Christ who question women in the Ministry when Christ, so they claim, did not call women as disciples.

> One of the things I have had to point out, according to the scriptures, is that when you are walking alongside of somebody, you are already involved. There is no need to call you or invite you to participate. And the women were already involved in Christ's Ministry. They were following Him. He had compassion upon them. He liberated them from demons and all kinds of sicknesses and diseases, and out of their own gratitude, they were already following Him. But much like we see in the Body of Christ in the world today, the men, as usual, were busy about their businesses. They were not paying attention to what Christ was saying and what He was teaching and to get their attention, He had to actually call them and say: "Come and follow me." But the

women were already following. And there are all kinds of scriptures that give evidence to what I am saying.

—Pastor Annette Taylor
Bethel Outreach Ministries
Maryland, USA/Liberia, West Africa

Moreover, the "out of the kitchen" directive is a powerful grand-slam against religious arguments that misinterpret scripture to uphold a patriarchal agenda of dominance and control. In addition, it supports a critical principle in feminist research and analysis on the continuing negative impact of the division of household labour that confines women's roles to the domestic sphere and then devalues those roles.

The issue of the division of household labour has been identified as a critical area of struggle in the home, not only because it reflects, replicates and supports the structural subordination of women in the society, but because, even if unconscious, it is a key strategy for limiting women's personal development and contribution outside of the home. Hence there is a corresponding negative impact on the ability to become financially independent. Recognition of this socio-economic dilemma represents an opportunity for the Church to design and implement models for restructuring for more egalitarian gender relations; however, it is an area in which the Church has failed by its own "head in the sand" approach, and its own stubborn reluctance to change. For example, within religious institutions, the ordination of women has become an on-going debate that drains energy, attention, focus, opportunity, and more significantly, action from the supreme commission of "Go, Tell!"

Walter Douglas, retired senior pastor of All Nations Church in Berrien Springs, Michigan, who in his capactiy as Chair of the Church History Department at Andrews University has been credited with training and organizing placement for many of the female pastors within the Seventh-day Adventist Church, points to Christ's model of inclusion.

> The Church needs to confront issues from theological, sociological and anthropological perspectives, not dodge them because of the fear of the inevitable conclusions. We cannot be the remnant church and be a racist Church. We cannot talk about justice and equality and discriminate on the basis of sex or ethnicity...**There is no systematic understanding of the reality of women's subordination, so there's no structured approach for dealing with it**...We have to move beyond a patchwork language of accommodation. Churches could better serve young women by taking them seriously and demonstrating that they have the power, capability, and resourcefulness to make an astounding contribution to the life and ministry of the church.[13]

We can see, then, how this interaction between Jesus, Martha and Mary represents another example of His Divine inclusion of women, in full knowledge of the strategic exclusion to which women would be subjected. His emphasis on the importance of Mary's interest is fully in sync with His other moves to draw attention to women, to foreground their actions, address their specific needs, and prepare them for the mission He intended.

Martha had already proven her own spiritual maturity. At the death of her brother, Lazarus, and just before Jesus brought him back to life, Martha held a most profound discussion with Jesus. First, she let loose two lightning bolts of faith. If Jesus had been there, she said, her brother would not have died. Secondly, and more importantly, she expressed her deep understanding and irrepressible faith.

---

13   Meryl James-Sebro, "What Women Need From Their Church," *Message* (March/April 1999).

> *But I know, that even now, whatsoever Thou wilt ask of*
> *God, God will give it Thee.*   *(John 11:22, KJV)*

What faith! In a popular slang of Trinidad and Tobago, "she made Him out!" Not only did she recognize His own Godliness, she recognized the source of His supreme authority and power, God the Father. In a response that appears almost too casual for the grief-laden Martha and the depth of the conversation, *Jesus* says:

> *Thy brother shall rise again.*   *(John 11:23, KJV)*

Again, displaying her full grasp of His mission and a deep understanding of His ministry, Martha replied:

> *I know that he shall rise again in the resurrection at the*
> *last day.*   *(John 11:24, KJV)*

Jesus was not surprised at the depth of her knowledge and understanding. He had spent enough time with these three friends, Martha, Mary and their brother, Lazarus, to know their individual spiritual level. And so, in a repeat of His engagement of the woman at the well in matters of deep spirituality, He revealed Himself.

> *I am the resurrection, and the life: he that believeth in*
> *me, though he were dead, yet shall he live. And whoso-*
> *ever liveth and believeth in me shall never die. Believest*
> *thou this?*   *(John 11:25–26, KJV)*

Jesus knew the answer. He had watched her spirit grow and her understanding deepen during their conversations on the many occasions He had been their house-guest. He knew Martha was ready. It was for this reason He had engaged Martha in a discussion of such spiritual weight and depth. He was pleased with her answer.

Yea, Lord: I believe that Thou are the Christ, the Son of God, which should come into the world.
(John 11:27, KJV)

Mary, however, needed more preparation. Then, fully in sync with His priorities, Martha walks away and whispers to her sister: "The Master is come, and calleth for thee." It was as though Martha knew she had passed her own test with flying colours, and that her sister, Mary, needed to attend many more lectures. Of course, the need to quickly and efficiently feed several hungry men moved such rationalization to the back burner.

Jesus had already known that Martha was well prepared and spiritually developed. He had made a public declaration of that fact by his mere action of meeting, greeting and having deep discussions with not only a woman, but one who had recent contact with the dead. These were serious violations of Jewish social, cultural and religious traditions. But, as was His intention, Jesus was breaking down those barriers for women, paving the way for the work that He knew only they could do. However, Mary had more preparatory work to do, and her workplace was out of the kitchen, at His feet.

Indeed it was Mary's eventual grasp of the immediacy of His message that enabled her to anoint Him for burial, while the disciples were still fussing with each other about their place in His Kingdom. Her own understanding deepened, and she received a spirit of discernment that forced her to return to the empty grave for further investigation. Moreover, she had attained a spiritual readiness that enabled Jesus to appear to her first, call her by name, and send her to preach His Resurrection to the other disciples. Sadly, the men could neither receive nor believe the message, perhaps because it came from a woman; perhaps because they were still preoccupied with competition for power and status. The state of disbelief and the devaluing of women appear to be linked and represent danger zones that counteract the will and intention of God, the negative effects of which ripple through the contemporary Church. They defy clear indications of the critical role intended for women in His Divine Plan, a role that goes beyond the secondary back benches to which women's participation has been reduced. What is more frightening, however, is the inherent danger of creating divisions, blocking the messages that women can bring, thwarting the spread of the Message, and holding back from others the love and saving grace of a Risen Saviour. Paul makes this danger clear to the early Church in Rome:

> *Now I beseech you, brethren, mark them which cause divisions and offences contrary to the doctrine which ye have learned; and avoid them. For they that are such serve not our Lord Jesus Christ, but their own belly; and by good words and fair speeches deceive the hearts of the simple.* (Romans 16:17-18, KJV)

A more modern translation underlines more specifically the danger to the Church of pursuing interests contrary to God's will and intention.

> *I beg you, my brothers, watch out for those who criticize and create problems and oppose the basic doctrines you've been taught. It is best for you to avoid them. These kinds of people are not really serving the Lord Jesus Christ but are serving their own interests. They speak kindly and acceptably to everyone and go around deceiving members who haven't had a chance to study as much as they have.* (Romans 16:17-18, CWV)

This is no idle warning. At the time of this writing, a small Baptist Church in upstate New York was thrown into disarray and division because a husband and wife team had been invited to an evening of praise and religious teaching. During the service there was laying of hands. Half of the Church attacked the Pastor for allowing such an abomination to occur at the Church. Church members who had invited the couple or supported them fled the Church, while the Pastor fumbled in despair and spiritual self-examination. Ironically, one member of the congregation wrote that he was much more interested in the message than the vessel used to convey that message, an instructive concept for most churches, regardless of denomination. The focus must be the message, not the medium. In fact, every possible medium must be used to ensure that the message effectively reaches target audiences. For certainly this was the intention of Jesus' point in supporting Mary's move beyond the kitchen to greater spiritual and intellectual development and fulfillment.

While many denominations are—albeit reluctantly—beginning to include women in ministry, the road has been fraught with pain, anguish and frustration. Lethargic, hierarchical structures have been all too slowly cutting through their own rust to make room for spirit-filled women with powerful messages, made more urgent by end-time crises. In the Seventh-day Adventist religion, the ordination of women was voted down after spirited discussion "in view of the possible risk of disunity, dissension, and diversion from the mission of the church."[14] The entire process is still packed with game-playing and compromises amidst on-going debates and discussion that seek to circumvent the core issues rather than bring about fundamental changes in culture and attitude. For example, one female pastor explained to me that she had been "inducted," not "ordained." Hence she could "reach" souls, impress the church leadership with traffic-jams at the altar in response to appeals, but she

---

14   Hyveth Williams, *Will I Ever Learn?: One Woman's Life of Miracles and Ministry* (Hagerstown: Review and Herald Publishing Association, 1996).

could not baptize them. That's a man's job…a ritual that many women pastors are still not permitted to perform. The issue of women pastors performing baptism continues to be as heated a debate as that of the ordination of women.

Dr. Hyveth Willimas, the first Black female Seventh-day Adventist pastor, has documented her own trials with tremendous courage, and has provided instructive lessons of the "straw men" erected about women's ministry and the ways in which women pastors are effectively destroying them. One such "straw man" is that women pastors are unable to effectively reach and win souls and will, in fact, turn people away from the church. During Pastor Williams' checkered rise in the religious hierarchy, many so-called Christian men threatened to leave the church she had been assigned. Many indeed left the church, or threatened to boycott services, while others actively protested and sought to revoke her appointments. Some even participated in "systematic harassment."

On one occasion, a visitor actually attacked her after church:

> You are an aberration. The leaders should shut this church down! You don't seem to have heard what I said. You women ought to be kicked out of the church; you're turning it into a farce![15]

That was only a visitor to the church. Actual members of one church to which she had been assigned proved they could go one step further.

> One Sabbath they stood up and interrupted the worship service, demanding to know by what biblical authority I was preaching and teaching in their church. One even declared that it was Eve who had brought sin into the world, and 'I will not sit back and allow you to bring sin into this church!' They refused to vote me in as an elder

---

15   Ibid., 127.

so that I could perform all of my pastoral duties. They disrupted board meetings with loud arguments, angry outbursts, and petulant walkouts. But they never told me by what authority they behaved in such a despicable manner.[16]

On yet another occasion Pastor Williams tells of arriving at a church to be the guest speaker. Shocked to find that "Pastor Hyveth Williams" was a woman, the elder openly expressed his despair.

I don't think that's going to work, he objected firmly. My daughter is here for the first time in a long time, and she's not going to listen to some woman.[17]

When it was finally agreed that Pastor Williams would be allowed to speak, she was given no introduction. Her friend who accompanied her to sing, however, was given a lengthy introduction.

The inference was clear. She was out of her place as a preacher; her friend in perfect place as a singer.

But God was with me. I gave it my best under the power of the Holy Spirit, and when I was finished the elder's daughter, who had long since dropped out of the Adventist Church, responded to an appeal to commit her life to Christ. That made her father so happy he invited us home for the most delicious vegetarian meal I have ever eaten.[18]

Women provide no less of a challenge, sometimes expressing more dissatisfaction and objection than the men themselves. We women have been so brainwashed into accepting this imposed position of subordination, that we harbour inner resentments of women who

16   Ibid., 176—77.
17   Ibid., 104.
18   Ibid., 105.

breakthrough these boundaries. Too often, instead of supporting these courageous sisters, we take up front-line positions in the on-going struggle against women. It is a position that men, individually, collectively and structurally depend upon as their most powerful ammunition.

In a Sabbath school class one morning, David and his seduction of Bathsheba was the topic of heated discussion. Some of the participants began to advance the suggestions that Bathsheba had actually strategically positioned herself in order to seduce King David.[19] This dramatic story that unfolds (2 Samuel 11 & 12) is a classic documentation of the serious implications of unequal gender relations between the powerful and the powerless. David, a powerful and popular king, and part-time voyeur, sees the beautiful Bathsheba bathing in the privacy of her courtyard garden. He flexes his royal power and kingly authority to get her to his bed...a command performance!

> *Then David sent messengers from the court to her house to tell her that the king would like to see her. That night she slept with him. Then early in the morning she returned home.* (2 Samuel 11:4, CWV)

We are not told whether she gleefully consented to the king's desire, or whether she was forced into the act. In contemporary society it is called sexual harassment at the very least; in the worst case scenario, rape. How could one of his subjects, the simple wife of his soldier and trusted bodyguard, refuse the powerful king...one who was powerful enough to manipulate the battlefield murder of her husband in order to cover his own sin and the shame of her resulting pregnancy?

---

19   It was the first time I had heard that partciular interpretation of David as victim, in the claws of Bathsheba, the alleged temptress. Sadly, it was not to be the last.

*A few weeks later she sent word to David telling him
that she was pregnant.* *(2 Samuel 11:5, CWV)*

Yet revisionist interpretations would position the powerless Bathsheba as temptress and seductress. My jaws were tight; but I was determined not to jump into the fray. However, Satan, as you well know, is clever and relentless. The gentleman sitting in front of me, who had his arm possessively around his wife, turned around, and of all people selected me to whisper conspiratorily: "You know, sometimes women can be devious; they will set you up!"

Apparently he had expected me to automatically agree with this revisionist notion of David as victim, falling prey to Bathsheba, allegedly a malevolent seductress. He received only a freezing stare, as I tried to bite my tongue and control my anger. He must have seen the flash in my eyes and a body position of stone disagreement, because when I saw him again about a month later, he sought me out to apologize for his misstatement. I was happy for the opportunity to sermonize on the need to more closely monitor the domineering activities of men who continue to victimize women and heap undeserved blame on them, while men stubbornly fail to own their own errors and to seek much-needed counseling. The main point of the incident, however, is that he had felt comfortable in considering another woman as an ally, thinking that I would very naturally and predictably support David over Bathsheba, an obvious victim in that story.

Given her own share of negative experiences with women who criticized her call to the ministry, Pastor Williams writes:

> ...I think we women are programmed to compete with and distrust each other. Where men network and

establish a "brotherhood" to look out for each other, we women often undermine each other by gossip, backbiting, and self-righteous attitudes that pit us against one another, instead of uniting our scanty resources to liberate ourselves from the tyranny of misogynism, no matter what form or ritual it takes.[20]

It appears, then, that we women ourselves need to understand the message of spiritual development and action within the context of balance that Jesus meant for all women…Mary, Martha, and 'Everywoman.' It is only then that we can apply His Purpose to our own lives, and understand the importance of supporting sisters who do the same. More critically, given the overwhelming majority of women in the world body of Christianity, women have much greater power than they are currently using to influence the content of the message and weigh in on the structure versus substance dilemma that the Christian Church is facing. But it takes a level of understanding of the issues, liberation from imposed ideas of male superiority and freedom from a perceived God-given right of men to dominate and manipulate the communication of His Word in order to first unshackle our own minds. Sadly, women have so internalized domination and subjugation, that we have been relied upon to wage battle against our own barrier-breaking sisters.

Indeed the world is depending on women to get out of the kitchen to take care of the business that is being betrayed by lust for power, greed, hypocrisy and general un-Godliness. Don't take my word for it. Ask Kenneth Lay of Enron, still smarting from the impact of Sherron Watkins, Vice President for Corporate Development, who ventured beyond the kitchen to the heat of big business. Thanks to her courage, determination, honesty and sense of fair play, a whole pot of corporate theft and abuse has

---

20   Ibid., 124-25.

been brought to the boil, overflowed, and then overturned. Thanks to this female whistle-blower, corporations will hopefully end the practice of cooking the books as a normal operating procedure to the detriment of unsuspecting employees and shareholders. But returning to spiritual matters, the pain of being woman today is one to which only another woman can have that visceral connection needed for effective ministry and spiritual healing. Some scholars believe that when the disciples were sent out two by two, there is the implication of a male and female team, in order that women could minister to the needs of other women.

Divine perception of the role of women beyond the kitchen is recorded and affirmed at the foot of the cross, where many women had gathered, <u>vigilant</u> to the very end, in spite of the threat to their lives. Among them were: Mary, the mother of Jesus, Mary Magdalene, Joanna and a few other women. And what is Jesus' final word to them?

> *Daughters of Jerusalem, weep not for me, but weep for yourselves and for your children. For behold, the days are coming, in the which they shall say, blesssed are the barren, and the wombs that never bare, and the paps which never gave suck. Then shall they begin to say to the mountains, Fall on us; and to the hills, Cover us.For if they do these things in a green tree, what shall be done in the dry?* (*Luke 23:28-31, KJV*)

In His Divine fore-knowledge of the pain, suffering, oppression and even death that would befall the world, almost exclusively by the hands of power-hungry men. But is Jesus also putting women on notice that those free of children would be in a more effective position to carry forth the hope of His return? Even though there is stark contradiction with Paul's observation that women will be saved in childbearing (*1 Tim 2:15*), certainly more weight must be given to the words of Jesus. In addition, Paul had earlier written to Timothy some of the texts most frequently-quoted and misinterpreted to validate male chauvinism:

> *Let the woman learn in silence with all subjection. But I suffer not a woman to teach, nor to usurp authority over the man, but to be in silence.*   *(1 Tim 2:11-12)*

Again, in his letter to the church in Corinth, Paul pleaded for order and decorum:

> *Let your women keep silence in the churches; for it is not permitted unto them to speak; but they are commanded to be under obedience as also saith the law. And if they will learn any thing; let them ask their husbands at home: for it is a shame for women to speak in the church.*
> *(1 Corinthinas 14:34-35)*

This one text has been pulled out of context to down play the roles of women and minimize their participation in the Church. I once heard a pastor on the radio advise a caller to leave and stay clear from any church in which women were in any leadership position, even giving Bible studies. Such action, he declared, was a direct affront to God's word, and showed that the church was operating in disobedience to God's word. It is indeed a complete reversal from earlier indications of women's financial and physical support and involvement in Jesus' ministry to "silencing" them in the Church. Let us go once more to Pastor Baird for an explanation of this Scripture.

> When the Apostle Paul spoke to the Church then, he was not speaking to us in this modern day. In the Jewish synagogue, when women were not allowed to speak. And even today in the Jewish synagogue, women are not seen as persons. They are nonentities. They're supposed to sit and

be quiet. And they are not even supposed to go into some temples. And so when they went into the temple. If Billy took in Sarah and she sat in the back, of course if you sit in the back in a low place, you can't really hear what the priest was saying, so they would shout across to each other's husband and say, "Well Billy, what is he saying?" And it was disruptive, which is understandable.

So the Apostle Paul said: Let them keep quiet in the church, and when they get home ask their husbands what has been said, and let them learn silently. And so men just pulled that out of context, without executing it correctly in terms of the Word, and just threw it at women for years, and women have been held back by that Scripture. And that's all that meant. Women, you're in the Temple, be silent in the Temple. When you get home and you don't understand what the Preacher was saying, ask your husband, Billy; ask your husband, Joe; ask your husband, Joseph, and he'll tell you what is being said. That's exactly what it meant, and that's something that men have used.

But now women are more educated, thankfully, and now they're going to Bible school, and now they're beginning to explain correctly the Word of God in the right context, and they're beginning to understand their role, and it's not to keep silent. Could you imagine what would happen in the Church today if women kept silent? You'd have no church, because the men are abandoning their roles in the Church, really, most of them, and most of them are just prim-priming. Thankfully the men are now returning back to Church, you're seeing a lot of men now back in the churches. But if the women had kept silent in the churches, we would not have…women kept the churches together. They kept the structures in place. You had a pastor, you had a thousand women, and maybe five men. Women were the Sunday School teachers. They were the Missionaries. They were the Heads of Departments. They were the ones that kept the church structure going, so if they had kept silent, we would have no church. Thankfully, the women didn't keep silent. They were not as visible in the public, but in the pew; they did their jobs quietly, and got it done. Men play their roles down, but there are powerful women in the Bible.

—Pastor Lucille Baird
Mt. Zion Ministries
Barbados, W.I.

Jesus' constant attention to the needs of women and His appointment of women to front-line positions at critical points of His ministry, in the face of the petty jealousies, rivalries and concern for power and status of the male disciples, evidence a *genderstanding* Jesus. In addition, it represents a powerful contradiction of Paul's words, which, it is widely agreed, have been taken out of context. One cannot overlook Judas' jealousy of the praise Jesus heaped on Mary who anointed Him for burial with an expensive spice, the funds for which had escaped Judas' deceptive mind and sticky fingers. In fact, some scholars believe that it was this jealousy that gave him the final push to betray Jesus to His enemies. Surely the recorded fact that the women waited, wept, wailed and watched at His Death, while the disciples slept, scattered and slipped out of notice into a locked room, must have caused lingering resentment that would inspire great efforts to "keep women in their place." It is a secondary place of passivity and victimization from which Jesus uplifted women, and to which many continue to try to return them, in spite of the spirit lashes suffered by the Church and society through this action. Translations or interpretations that promote hierarchical structures and discriminatory practices certainly do not reflect the egalitarianism with regard to gender, race, ethnicity, creed, age and national origin, which Jesus modeled consistently through His Ministry and His Life.

At the time of this writing the Conference of Roman Catholic Bishops is meeting in the United States to discuss the protection of children from paedophile priests and a Church hierarchy more concerned about preserving its structure, tradition and image than protecting powerless children. In addition, pervasive abduction of children by sexual predators brings new meaning to this "blessing" of barrenness, to which Jesus referred, as quoted earlier. This interpretation in no way devalues the importance of mothers and their esteemed roles in society. It does, however, force us to rethink the emphasis placed on the importance of women *only* as mothers. It challenges the masculinist notion of women's exclusivity in the nurturing of children. It also examines the confinement of women to a mothering role that precludes self-development, participation or leadership in any area outside the domestic sphere and its related activities of caring and nurturing. Moreover, it directs our gaze to the role of fatherhood and its indirect and distanced function which society appears to accept and encourage.

Greater balance of roles in day-to-day household management would certainly permit a more positive presence of the father figure. This balance would also model the love and attention of God, the supreme Father. At the same time, it would allow the space and time for the positive development of women in areas beyond domestic requirements, thus benefitting women, the family, the Church and, by extension, society. In contrast to this Divine strategic involvement of women, the body of Christ is burdened with a man-made agenda to side-line or devalue women's contributions.

> Modern day man thinks that Jesus didn't have a role for women, and that's unfortunate. Perhaps deliberately, they do not see, or fail to emphasize the role of the women around Jesus, and all the women that stood with

Him as significant. They saw it as just a very minor role they play. But looking at it now, they were major roles. Because in every church there are different ministries. Everybody can't be a preacher, everybody can't be a pastor. If you don't clean the bathrooms, then the preacher would be in pain, because when a person leaves the church and the anointing upstairs and comes downstairs to the bathroom and it's dirty, they may turn around and not come back, no matter how good the preacher is. So everybody's role is important. I think that modern day man has played down the role of the women around Jesus because they don't see the significance.

—Pastor Lucille Baird
Mt. Zion Ministries
Barbados, W.I.

That is in the physical and material realm. In the spiritual realm, the Church continues to be greatly affected.

In spite of all of the gifts that are in the female, the woman has not been allowed to come forth. And so the Church is being robbed of the gifts, the skills, the abilities and the resources that are there, lying dormant and played down and it's really sad, because where the woman is allowed to be free and to minister to her full potential, that Church can grow, that Church can take the nation. That Church can be anything that God will have it to be, because everybody's part is so vital in the body. And so, if you have the woman in the Church and she's not allowed to be who she'll have to be, that Church is not functioning in its full capacity.

—Pastor Lucille Baird
Barbados, W.I.

Indeed it is a stark reminder of Paul's warnings that:

These kinds of people are not really serving the Lord Jesus Christ but are serving their own interests. They

speak kindly and acceptably to everyone and go around
deceiving members who haven't had a chance to study
as much as they have.   *(Romans 16:17-18, CWV)*

In practical terms, however, the serving of male suprem-
acy interests links male dominance and control to
women's economic impoverishment and their lack of
social and political empowerment. This has implications
for not only discrimination, but many of the crimes of
violence that make the home unsafe for defenseless
women and children. Primarily there is a sense of
unrestricted power that creates and sustains men as physical and emotional bullies of women, even as it chips away
at the self-esteem of women, leaving frustration, dependence and a sense of dis-empowerment. It is this sense of
dis-empowerment that makes women easy prey to male
dominance and bullying in domestic and public spaces.
More critically, the widespread acceptance of women's
subjugation restricts the ability of the Church to come to
the aid of women and children when victimized in their
homes. The homes of pastors, preachers, and religious
elders are not immune to domestic violence. In fact, recent
research shows that incidents of incest and domestic
violence are prevalent in the homes of Christian conserva-
tives, and draw a striking correlation between the level of
religious conservatism and domestic violence.

Domestic violence activists have held male-dominated,
authoritarian structures responsible for *not only* violence in
the home, *but also* the secrecy with which it is usually
shrouded. Recent revelations of pervasive paedophilia in
the U.S. Roman Catholic Church point to the ways in
which intricate and deliberate attempts to protect powerful structures of abuse become institutionalized and fester
into continuing abuse of victims. Further, there is deep
frustration with the religious guidance abused women

have traditionally received, which further confuses and often intensifies women's victimization.

> We have had a sizeable proportion of people reporting violence from fundamentalist religious groups, wherever they are. With the Christian ones, we have unfortunately had a number of reports from the wives of pastors, and other very fundamentalist religious organisations. It's very much like a Hindu or a Muslim deal where the male is the authority and the head of the house and can do literally anything he wants, and punishes as he sees fit in order to discipline the family. So we get a fair number of abusive cases there. Sort of like with the police. You know there is a high level of battering amongst police and people in the regiment, because of the same authoritarian kind of structures that they are programmed to work within, because religious organizations are very authoritarian in terms of their structures
>
> —Senator Diana Mahabir, Executive Director
> The Coalition Against Domestic Violence
> Trinidad, W.I.

These authoritarian structures were also linked to incest:

> They feel they have a right to their daughters' bodies because…One of them said that he felt it was his duty as a father to instruct his daughter in how to develop her sexuality. And I remember another case where his attitude was, 'Well you know, I'm the head of the household, and they all belong to me and must do as I say.' And they don't feel any guilt at all about it.
>
> —Senator Diana Mahabir, Executive Director
> The Coalition Against Domestic Violence
> Trinidad, W.I.

Religious authoritarian structures have been grounded in one of the most hotly debated scriptures from Paul's letter to the Ephesians:

> *Wives, submit yourselves unto your own husbands, as unto the Lord. For the husband is the head of the wife, even as Christ is the head of the Church: and He is the Saviour of the body.* *(Ephesians 5:22-23, KJV)*

This scripture has indeed been taken out of context to terrorize women and children in their homes, in the workplace, and shockingly, even in the Church. One disenchanted woman described an affair with a senior church elder. A powerful, successful doctor, he used this male-centric concept of submission to manipulate her back into the life of fornication from which she had struggled to free herself. "How can I marry you if I'm not sure that you will submit to me in marriage because you will not submit to me now," he argued. Needless to say, he had somehow bent the scripture to mean submitting to his bed. She found the strength to withdraw from his brand of submission only when the Spirit led her to his house one afternoon to find that he had yet another sister in bed-time submission.

Perhaps the very best example of the moral and Godly right to refuse to submit is found within the Bible itself. It is difficult to maintain a balanced view of the reason that, in general, sermons on this text de-emphasize the right of non-submission. Ironically, the text is frequently used to chastise women into obedience to men. It is the story of Queen Vashti, as told in the Old Testament Book of Esther.

The King is celebrating with his boys, drinking and having a grand ole' time. In his drunken stupor, he decides to show off his beautiful wife, and sends for the elegant Queen Vashti. In her wisdom, Queen Vashti sends an alarming response: "Sorry, buddy, I'm not coming." Of the many times I have heard this scripture used in sermons, I have only heard support of Queen Vashti twice: the first time by a female preacher; the second time by an enlightened male pastor. However, it is the female pastor, who contextualized the scene to reveal that the King might actually have been asking his Queen to dance naked before his friends so that they could see her astounding beauty. Even in a less extreme version, the King might have been asking Queen Vashti to appear unveiled, which in those days would have been tantamount to appearing nude...as it very much is in some mid-Eastern cultures today.

Given the drunkeness of his friends, and the complete abandonment of good sense, taste and judgment on the part of the king, Vashti knows that she could very well be the sexual object of an alcohol-induced orgy. Exercising exemplary wisdom, she refuses to appear. The king is naturally scandalized at her display of disobedience, perhaps more so embarrassed before his friends. Some scholars advance the argument that the King later came to his senses, recognized his error, and was willing to "forgive" Queen Vashiti whom he loved, and whose beauty was extraordinary. However, his male confidants and subjects grumbled that they would never again be able to "control" their women if the king could not control his. Thus, he succumbed to the pressure, and banished Queen Vashti.

All of the supporting arguments have been represented in the response of one Christian woman:

> Don't talk to me about submitting if you can't do your part. Christ's love is complete and unconditional. If men truly do their part women will have no difficulty submitting.[21]
>
> —Dr. Vonda Douglas
> Gainesville, Florida

---

21   Meryl James-Sebro, "What Woman Need From Their Church," *Message* (March/April, 1999).

This observation quickly puts the entire argument into perspective. For the complete submission of men to Christ's Will could never be synonymous with the abuse of power and the control and domination in the home that are so directly linked to violence against women and children. But the focus on this one verse, Eph. 5:22–23, in a message intended to ensure love and a balance of power is overwhelming proof of the danger of faulty interpretations and wrongful emphases that serve male supremacist interests over God's Will. What is more insidious, is the deliberate exclusion of the text that precedes these verses in order to prevent misreading and misinterpretation.

> *Submitting yourselves one to another in the fear of God.*
> *(Ephesians 5:21, KJV)*

Or, in more easily understood English:

> *Show a submissive spirit to one another for Christ's sake* *(Ephesians 5:21, CWV)*

This one line carefully and knowingly introduces the elements of mutual respect, equality and balance as ground rules for a covenant relationship. It is, however, the one line that is strategically excluded in the frequent quoting of the Ephesians text that supposedly supplies Biblical support for male dominance and control. Domestic violence survivors often lament these macho, authoritarian attitudes with which they're forced to battle when seeking safe harbour from religious organizations.

> The morning when I left, he got up with the intention that he was going to kill me, the two children, and himself. And I went to the police station and report it, and the first thing the police asked me is what I do the man. Because I had to do the man something for him to behave like that. So I had lost faith in, you know. Years

before I had gone through a situation with him and lawyers and divorce. When I left the lawyer's office, he said if I divorce him today, I'll be dead the next day, so I never bothered. And when you go to the priest and everybody, everybody telling you 'pray, is yuh husband.' So I get fed-up after a time, you know, so I just lost faith in everything kind of way, in terms of that.

—Domestic violence survivor
Trinidad, W.I.[22]

In a training video, titled "Broken Vows: Religious Perspectives on Domestic Violence,"[23] Jewish and Christian religious leaders lament the silence and inaction with which churches and synagogues have responded to domestic violence. Moreover, refusal to deal with the problem—often with great insensitivity and blame-placing on the woman—has kept religious institutions from providing a safe haven for victims of domestic violence. Yet, very often, religious institutions represent the only places of refuge and comfort. Surely this should be a critical part of their Ministry if they're in tune with the ugly revelation of violence against women as a global phenomenon that crosses boundaries of class, ethnicity, age, religion and national origin.

One night he got drunk. My father came home drunk. Stoned. And just chased everybody out of the house. It was night, about 3 o'clock in the morning, and we just ran away. He was drinking, and he actually woke my two children sleeping with me on the bed, and just dragged them out of the bed and said: 'Allyuh get out of meh house, allyuh in meh way,' and just throw the children out. And these two little boys just run out the road crying, middle of the night, dark night, and the

---

22   Meryl James-Sebro, *Flagwomen: The Struggle Against Domestic Violence in Trinidad and Tobago*, (Ann Arbor, MI: Bell and Howell Information and Learning Company, 2001), UMI Microform 3007926.

23   A production of The Center for the Prevention of Sexual and Domestic Violence, Safe Haven Ministries. Seattle, WA. Tel: (206) 634-1903.

neighbours took them in. I ran and stayed by uhm Pastor Kiel. I was going to Church. I was going to New Life Ministries, a Pentecostal Church, because they were…Pastor Kiel and his wife…they had come here to pioneer, so they were looking to assist and help people. They were Americans. White. And they took us in. We stayed there for some time.

—Domestic violence survivor
Trinidad, W.I.[24]

Still religious institutions have been slow to make the connection between man-made, masculinist theology that promotes power and control over women and unequal socio-economic and political conditions that continue to haunt women in every area of their lives. They have been even more lethargic in guiding discussions in the Church to be more proactive in recognizing and institutionalizing strategies for addressing domestic violence. Such strategies would include built-in preventive measures, including the review of Church doctrines that reflect interests influenced by society, not modeled by the compassion and egalitarianism of Jesus Christ.

On the other hand, women rely on their faith and relationship with God for the strength and strategy to survive.

But I never gave up faith in God, and I think that's what kept me going all these years. That kept me going all those years, and still have me on meh two feet. God's grace.

—Domestic violence survivor
Trinidad, W.I.[25]

With gender-based violence and discrimination, as with racism, the Church has indeed lost face and its leadership

---

24   Meryl James-Sebro, Ibid.
25   Ibid.

place in helping to set and preserve a moral tone in society, primarily because of its lack of compassion. This is the compassion that was central to Jesus' Life, Message and Ministry, and which women are wired to impart. It is, perhaps, the most crucial loss to Church and society.

> I think we've lost our compassion when we refuse to get women involved. One of the things that shows up a lot about Jesus in the Scriptures is His compassion. He looked at somebody, and He had compassion; and then He would try to help them. I think that's an apt description of women. Women have an innate sense of compassion, and they will reach out to somebody who looks like they're going down and under just by that sense of compassion. I think when we refuse to allow women to be in leadership roles, we're just denying our church that role of compassion, which could encircle so many people that are being lost. One of the things that I noticed in my ministry, which is still very young, is how the children—I say children, but not meaning 4 and 5—how the young people run to me. That always catches my attention… I do believe it's that compassion…that touch. Sometimes I see one of them looking a little sad or something, we're not having any major big discussion, but I'll go and I'll hug them, and I'll probably say just a few words, and I'll go on and next time we'll follow up. And I think that compassion is catching. It's drawing. It has a drawing influence. So to not have that could make your work in ministry as a male a lot more difficult…Males sometimes just don't have it…So to me we deny our Church…you will always see the response of the young people to somebody who has that touch of compassion.
>
> —Pastor Brenda Billingy
> Bladensburg Seventh-day Adventist Church
> Maryland

Jesus' "out of the kitchen" message to Martha guides us beyond the stirring of pots to the stirring of Mary's thirst for learning and spiritual development, with a powerful and compassionate direction for women. The message is not simply to balance domesticity with personal development. It is to understand and accept the responsibility of learning...about Him, His Ministry, and the many different roles to which He has called women. It holds a warning to stay connected to Him, remaining focused and avoiding the distractions of a male dominated world that seeks to advance its own masculinist, hierarchical interests that contradict His teaching and His mission. It is to follow the model of Mary, His mother, in her acceptance of a radical call on her life.

> But I think that the women of God now must begin to look and to revisit the scene, revisit the Bible, and begin to see their roles in a more significant way, and not allow modern day man to play down the roles that they have to play at the Hand of the Master and the Church, especially the modern day Church.
>
> —Pastor Lucille Baird
> Mt. Zion Ministries
> Barbados, W.I.

In spite of the struggle within themselves and against male-dominated restrictions, women throughout the Christian Church are beginning to answer the call on their lives to pursue functions beyond the kitchen of a role-restricted Church. While the male-dominated Church lingers in its preoccupation with structure, women are going to the substance of the message, taking hold of the commission to "Go Tell." In a seeming re-play of the difference in perspectives, understanding and action during Jesus' Ministry, men remain trapped in the vise of hierarchical traditions and power that subjugate women. Women, on the other hand have broken through the barriers of a restricting Christianity that challenges their right to answer the very call of God on their lives. In the same way that Jesus touched the woman with the spirit of infirmity that had kept her bent over with a curved spine, the touch of Jesus is straightening women up and out, leaving them erect, passionate, prepared, freed and fired for action. It is a touch that restores vibrant power to the brittle, osteoporosic bones of oppressive traditions.

> If we will let ourselves be open to the Spirit, I think a lot more will happen for us in terms of Kingdom-Building. The women who seem to be focussed, true to their call and demonstrate the fruits of the Spirit, those women are touching thousands of people.
> —Pastor Brenda Billingy
> Bladensburg Seventh-day Adventist
> Maryland

In a weird twist of fate that is grounded in faith, some women are beginning to consider exclusion from the organized Church a blessing in disguise, because of the freedom it allows and the energy that it permits them to direct to more Kingdom-building pursuits. They replace concern over ordination and upward mobility in the Church structure with a commitment to remain God-connected, "purpose-focused." and obedient.

> I read an article the other day of this woman in, I think it was in India. She is a lay minister, not part of the Church structure at all, but she just decided this is what God wants her to do. That woman is baptizing people by the thousands. They still have problems bringing her in the Church, even after all that. But her focus is; 'God didn't send me to the Church.' She is an Adventist, but her mind-set is: God's commission was "Go To." It wasn't "Come and Sit." And if we take that commission seriously, "Go To" all the way, these women will begin to clean up. I think a lot of times we stay struggling with the Church structure, and we stay encased and enclosed there. But if we are true to the commission of "Go and teach the gospel," this world will be touched. There's not

a question. There are women doing it already, and our society will be different, simply because of the traits that women have that are so different and unique to what men possess.

—Pastor Brenda Billingy
Bladensburg Seventh-day Adventist
Maryland

Yet in many cases, some of the most severe opposition to women in leadership roles in the Church comes from women themselves. Not only in criticizing and withholding support from women religious leaders, but in self-censorship that limits God's call on their own lives. It is precisely for this reason that Jesus urged vigilance in protecting the thirst for greater knowledge and the enthusiasm for inspired action.

Mary hath chosen that good part, which shall not be taken away from her. (*Luke 10:42, KJV*)

Unfortunately, unfortunately, sometimes the worst pressure you can get will come from your female counterparts. I just chalk that up to be brainwashed women. There's one female that I talked to the other day who feels that she should be an elder, like God is talking to her about accepting that role, but the mind-set is…more trouble than you can even think of…her mind-set. Her own mind-set. So in essence, it's a battle against your own self…how awesome could that be that you choose to battle against God in your own mind? I mean what is that? But the struggle is real. And my response was: "I can't tell you what to do, because you need to be convinced of God. Because once you accept that call, there's going to be a whole lot of other stuff that you're going to have to deal with. And if you're not confident that this is what you're supposed to be doing, it'll take you all under. So, I can't tell you this is what women are supposed to be doing. I can just tell you be sure that you're confident of the calling of God on your life.

—Pastor Brenda Billingy
Bladensburg Seventh-day Adventist
Maryland

Pastor Billingy's words found resonance with my own self-doubt and soul searching in the writing of this book, until I completely surrendered to His Will. As a Christian feminist, a concept which many understandably find a paradox in itself, daring to be perceived as criticizing the Body of Christ, was indeed daunting. But it is the conspiracy of silence that has become more threatening, and the attempt to turn a deaf ear to my own Spirit-led command to "Go, Write!" that became more frightening. There is no telling how instrumental and effective Christian women can be when we prioritize the Divine "Out of the Kitchen" call on our own lives over the comforts of traditions that cloud our vision, muffle our voices and stifle the new breath and breadth that women bring to Christ's mission on earth.

Genderstanding Jesus:

Questions for Reflection, Discussion and Action

Chapter 5

1). How do you interpret the Biblical command of the submission of women?

2). How can the Church be more pro-active in addressing incest and violence against women?

3). How do you feel about women in leadership roles in the Church?

4). How do you feel about the ordination of women?

5). What are the roles of Spirit-led women in the face of a Church restricted by male supremacist traditions?

6). What is the image of the Church as modeled by the Life and Ministry of Jesus?

7). What is your own "Out of the Kitchen" direction? Discuss strategies/obstacles for obeying it.

GENDERSTANDING JESUS

Chapter 6

WOMEN OF SUBSTANCE

While she is not often given credit for it, one woman who got out of the kitchen was Mrs. Zebedee. Right out of the kitchen she got. I could see her wiping her hands on her apron and smoothing back her hair, wrapping her shawl around her as she went to see this Jesus Man, to seek the interests of her sons, James and John. Mother Zebedee was not playing. She got right into the mix. How amused Jesus must have been! Her enthusiasm and goal may have been misguided, and she may have displayed a tremendous error in judgment, but you have to admire her *chutzpah*, strength of purpose and determination.

Remember, however, that Mrs. Zebedee was led by the murmurings of her overly ambitious sons, with their eyes on material status and earthly goals. She must have been sick of hearing her sons moaning, complaining and griping, worrying about their "rightful place." So, she decided to take the bull by the horns. Competition and concern for status stand out in the behavior of the disciples, in stark contrast to the compassion, collaboration and cooperation which the women exhibited. How different from the women who remained at the foot of the cross, vigilant to the end, coming back before sunrise to find the opened and emptied grave.

The appropriate ordering of priorities, having the right perspective, staying focused, connected and obedient continue to emerge as lessons from a close-up view of the women who surrounded Jesus. Moreover, the women accepted the challenge of total surrendering to God's will, as modeled by Jesus Christ Himself. Total submission to God remains a daunting challenge for today's Christian woman, if she is called to go beyond accepted traditional roles to front-line positions of Christian leadership and activism. Those whom God calls, however, He first prepares, strengthens and sends support, often along with confirmation of the task ahead. How prepared and strengthened was Mary, the mother of Jesus, in the face of what must have been the hottest bit of gossip of all time? And then came the Divine-led support from fiancé, Joseph, and confirmation from cousin Elizabeth, bearing her own bundle of hope and joy.

The ever-present Mary Magdalene, Joanna, Mary, the mother of James, Simone and a group of other women were prepared first thing that Sunday morning. Their preparation allowed them to be in the right place at the right time. Hence, they were selected to carry the message of the Risen Christ. But, no one believed them. Hiding in a room, immobilized by fear of the Jews who had just cruci-fied their Friend and Master, perhaps still arguing about how places of honour should be divided among them, the male disciples did not believe the women. It is the same challenge with which the majority of today's religious leaders are faced: the challenge of dismantling barriers of unbelief with respect to the work women have been called to do; tearing down the pillars of racism, sexism, and ageism that prop up structural inequities and hold back the outflow of compassion, concern for equality, social justice and the accompanying economic and spiritual poverty.

Loyalty and faithfulness were not strangers to these women. Some of them had been healed by Jesus. Mary Magdalene, we know for sure. Joanna was actually the wife of Chuza, an officer in King Herod's court. What courage! Along with Susanna and others, they had been following Jesus. But they weren't mere followers.

> *They ministered unto Him of their substance.*
>
> *(Luke 8:3, KJV)*

In plain English:

> *They used their resources to help Jesus and His disciples*
>
> *(Luke 8:3, CWV)*

Business women, entrepreneurs and property owners, these women were sponsors of His Ministry. Why is this such a well-guarded secret? Not only were they women of substance, they used that substance to take care of Jesus and His group of transients and to further His Work. Is this a Jesus that would recognize, understand and utilize women's skills, talents and resources in His earthly ministry, then sideline, subjugate and silence women in His Church today? These women did not go away after His ascension to Heaven. In the face of continued terrorism, they used their homes to house churches and to continue His work. Lydia, a successful business woman who traded in expensive purple cloth, invited Paul and his fellow-travellers to stay with her and her family at her home in Philippi. Paul sends greetings to the Roman women, making sure to mention Phoebe, as a sister and servant[26] of the church in, Cenchrea and Mary, who:

> *...bestowed much labour on us*   *(Romans 16:6, KJV)*

He was careful to include in his greetings Priscilla, Aguila, Mary, Julia, Olympas, Tryphaena, Tryphosa.

---

26   Many Biblical scholars interpret the word "servant" to mean "priest/pastor."

...two women who never stop working for Christ, and to Persis, whom we love and who works so hard for the Lord. (Romans 16;12, CWV)

It is in this very note that Paul begs his brothers:

...watch out for those who criticize and create problems and oppose the basic doctrines you've been taught. It is best for you to avoid them. (Romans 16:17, CWV)

These women not only gave of their substance as recorded in Luke, but they represented and provided the spiritual substance of the early Church. Many scholars have argued that women were more visibly involved in leadership roles in the early Church than they are today. This is a significant fact, because of the link between the invisibility of women at leadership levels, the dearth of feminine energy and the silence with which the male-dominated leadership responds to domestic violence and all of its ugly forms, implications and effects.

Imprinted in the Old Testament are the footsteps of many powerful women that cannot be erased. Deborah, for example, was the only female judge and governor in Israel, ruling, interestingly enough, at the height of her country's evil, rebellion and disobedience (*Judges 4:4-24*). A powerful woman who prophesied over the state of her nation, she commanded an attack on her nation's enemies, after hearing from the Lord. Here again we see the importance of Godly women listening, not to the worldly words of men, but to the voice of God, and speaking under the authority of God. However, it is only through a sustained connection with God that one can recognize the direction of God, speaking within in that still, small voice, or through the words of men...and women.

The brave Barak must have been a fearless and trustworthy warrior, for Deborah commissioned him to execute this important God-directed mission to destroy the mighty and evil Sisera. Barak would be considered one of today's macho men. In fact, his name meant "thunderbolt," and he's listed among the heroes of faith in *Hebrews (11:32)*. But macho man Barak was not intimidated by Deborah's power, and certainly not above taking his orders from a woman. In fact, so confident was he, not in her word, but the **source** of her words, that he said unashamedly: "If you go with me, I will go; but if you don't go with me, I won't go. *(Judges 4:8)*. What is historically interpreted as Barak's timidity, I interpret as his admirable resistance to linking his masculinity to dependence on a woman's leadership. The source of Deborah's direction, which he knew as the one true God, was more important than his male ego. His ego was dependent on God; therefore, he could accept the guidance of a Godcentric woman. How the Church cries out for more Baraks! And how much like God to make a point of using the strong, powerful male figure of Barak to give support and validity to Deborah's reign.

But this astute Queen Bee wanted to make sure that Barak understood the deal, and that his ego could withstand the test.

> *I will surely go with thee: notwithstanding the journey that thou takest shall not be for thine honour; for the Lord shall sell Sisera into the hand of a woman. And Deborah arose and went with Barak to Kedesh.*
> *(Judges 4:9, KJV)*

I have deliberately used the King James version for this scripture, since it has been subject to many different interpretations, most of them supporting a perception of Barak's timidity, cowardice, and even lack of faith in the Lord's word. However, my own *genderstanding* of the text points to four powerful messages: 1). Barak 's preoccupation with the mission and its success, not personal glory. His focus on his country's victory, not the few seconds of CNN-like fame. 2) The fearlessness of a powerful woman of God, ready to take aggressive front-line action, once it has been ordained by a faithful God, with whom she sustains a deep relationship. 3). Barak's sense of protection in the company of a woman of God. 4). A God that is willing to hand over a powerful victory to a woman in order to support and validate, in His usual dramatic way, the leadership of Godcentric women. It is indeed high drama. For although Deborah accompanies Barak, the arch enemy Sisera dies, not at her own powerful hands, but at the hands of an ordinary peasant woman, Jael.

As the saga unfolds, when Sisera, the feared captain of the enemy, abandons his army under attack from Barak, he flees into Jael's tent for hiding. Sisera knew that the traditions prevented any man but Jael's husband to enter the tent, making it a safe hiding place, at least long enough to give him a chance to rest from the vicious battle he had just escaped. Moreover, Jael's husband was a good friend of Barak's enemy, King Jabin, so Sisera knew that he was in friendly quarters. What he did not know, however, was that Jael's politics must have differed radically from those of her husband, who was thought to have informed Sisera of all of Barak's military manoeuvres.

Jael presented the picture of Ms. Hospitality herself. Sisera asked for water, Jael gave him milk, ordinarily a prized commodity, but a particular treasure in the heat of battle. She covered him with her best rug and probably smiled sweetly. Confident that she had his back and would follow his orders to deny that anyone was hiding in her tent, Sisera fell into a deep exhausted sleep. But while he slept comfortably, Jael literally took the situation into her own hands and nailed his skull to the ground with a tent peg. It must not escape us that the ruse of sweetness, hospitality and grace which Jael used are those usually associated with the deceitful and devious qualities which men so often associate with women, and which they feel disqualify women from leadership positions. Jael, however, makes a powerful case for the strategic use of God-anointed feminine wiles and guile under the authority of God. It is the proven concept of catching more flies with honey than with vinegar. In addition, that day she confirmed God's words, through Deborah, that the honour of the victory would go to a woman, giving further credibility and validity to Deborah's reign. It is a secret too quietly kept, but we serve a gender-sensitive God!

Another woman of substance served as a model of passive resistance and action in the face of outright barbarism for Christian women who went to Iraqi to serve as human shields during the USA "pre-emptive" invasion of March, 2003. Rizpah is only one of the heroic women of the Bible, so rarely memorialized in sermons, but from whom Iraqi Christian women drew strength, hope and courage as they prayed for their own lives, the safety of their children and husbands and peace for their land.

In the Biblical drama near the end of the reign of King David, the land is riddled with drought and famine because of King Saul's senseless, cold blooded killing of the Gibeonites. In an attempt to make amends and rid this curse, King David agrees to allow seven of Saul's male descendants to be executed and their bodies hung publicly in Saul's hometown. Among them are two sons of Rizpah's, one of Saul's concubines. She is pained over the death of her son, a searing pain that is heightened by the lingering shame, indignity and public dishonour of their exposed bodies. They have not only been denied a decent burial, their bodies are left to the mercy of vultures and wild animals. Ms. Rizpah is forced to take drastic action. And so this courageous, grief-stricken mother takes her mourning clothes, spreads them on a rock beside the bodies of her sons, and sits and sits and sits, day and night, for weeks and months, guarding the dead bodies from the further indignity of being eaten by animals. This heroic woman of substance, hidden in the pages of the Old Testament, took protest to the purest and highest level, highlighting the superpower of one woman in the face of state power, arrogance and un-Godliness. We are told that her action pierced the heart of the King.

> *When David heard about the honour Rizpah gave her sons, he was moved with compassion and greatly sympathized with her.* *(2 Samuel 21:11, CWV)*

King David, forced to take another look at his own actions and his own inhumanity, ordered the bones of Saul, Jonathan and other men whose bodies had been similarly dishonoured, to be dug up and given honourable burials in their home towns. Rizpah's sole action of quiet and persistent protest enabled the bodies of her sons to be decently buried in the ancestral tomb with their father, King Saul. Centuries later, Mahatma Gandhi and Dr. Martin Luther King would employ the same soul force to confront and counter physical force, injustice and aggression. More significantly, Rizpah rescued her King from his own dehumanization that filtered through the land. She became the motivating force for the restoration of God's grace and favour on her people.

> *They buried them in the tomb of Kish, Saul's father, and the Lord allowed the rains to return and refresh the drought-stricken land* *(2 Samuel 21;14, CWV)*

There is a powerful lesson here for those who would ignore, underestimate, or deem insignificant the power of relentless mother-love, feminine energy and women's contribution to development and peace. There is encouragement for women to use this power of stubborn love to combat male arrogance, pride and senseless warmongering. And, there is a responsibility of the Church to support and follow the leadership of women in their quest for human rights, peace and the eradication of poverty and injustice.

The Old Testament guides us to Abigail as another woman of substance. She is described as a wise, intelligent and beautiful woman, but married to a mean, violent, foolish, but wealthy landowner. Indeed, his name Nabal meant "fool," thus confirming the ancient belief of persons assuming the characteristics of their name. It took the wise actions of a sweet-tongue woman like Abigail to reverse the fiery wrath of David and his army against the foolish Nabal. But don't take my word for this story of the intervention of a wise and perceptive woman in the midst of a male power struggle. Read it for yourself in *1 Samuel 25*.

Having guarded the large flock of the wealthy Nabal, David thought it only fair that Nabal bestow kindness on him by feeding his soldiers, who were tired, weary and hungry from hiding from the relentless, vindictive and equally foolish King Saul. But the arrogant Nabal refused, relaying a heap of insults through David's men. David reacted in kind, swearing to wipe out Nabal and every male in his household. A diligent servant quickly brought the situation to Abigail's attention, confident that she would use her woman-wisdom to stall the consequences of her husband's folly. Without a moment's hesitation Ms. Abigail rose to the occasion, deliberately strategizing her intervention in the battle of male egos between her self-centered, hot-headed husband and the future King David.

Unknown to her husband, she packed a figurative war chest of bread, fresh grape juice, smoked lamb, bushels of roasted wheat, and even included dessert of hundreds of fresh raisins and figs. She loaded them on donkeys and sent them ahead with servants, bringing up the rear with her own deadly arsenal of charm, wit, intelligence and beauty. On meeting the angry David and his band of warriors, Abigail delivers a speech fit for the United Nations Security Council in any of its most sensitive, war-stopping attempts. She accepts the blame for her husband's senseless actions during her absence, and takes responsibility, since she was not there to interject some intelligence in a situation that her admittedly foolish husband was incapable of doing:

> *I wasn't there, so I didn't have chance to explain things to your young men when they came.*
> *(1 Samuel 25:25, CWV)*

With skilled diplomacy, she reminds David of the Divine guidance that prevented him from staining his hands with the blood of his enemy, King Saul, expressing confidence that the Divine force would take care of enemies such as her foolish husband, who was unworthy of David's murderous intentions. Abigail then presents her generous gifts; but she is not finished. Her strategic flattery continues: fluent, eloquent, complimentary, even forecasting his destiny of greatness, rulership and his Divine protection. She warns against the guilt of having innocent blood on his hands as he rose to glory, all because of one man's foolishness. She peppers him with praises, and, in a winning *coup de grace* that would cover all future bases, she expresses the hope that he would remember her kindness when he was enjoying the tremendous blessings of the Lord, which she is sure were to be his. The fierce David became putty in her hands.

> *"Praise be to the God of Israel who sent you to meet us. May He bless you for your good judgment and for*

stopping me from shedding innocent blood."
(1 Samuel 25:32-33, CWV)

Abigail returned home to find the foolish Nabal in a drunken stupor. When he learnt of her assertive action, his ego was shattered, in spite of the fact that her intervention changed David's murderous intentions against him. He suffered a massive heart attack and died ten days later, a characteristically foolish death. On hearing that this wise and beautiful woman was widowed, David, in a brilliant move, found one way of harnessing her wisdom for future use. He married her.

...And if I perish, I perish.   *(Esther 4:16)*

These are the words of another courageous Old Testament woman of substance who used the exalted position in which God had placed her to save her people. Her story begins with the banishment—some say she was killed— of Queen Vashti, which I related in the preceding Chapter. Esther wins a beauty competition that has been carefully staged in order to find a worthy replacement for the defamed Queen Vashti. Her prize is not only a crown, but a real throne, as bride of the powerful King Ahasuerus. She keeps her Jewish identity a top secret, until she learns of the planned extinction of the Jews through the designs of the wicked Haman. Supported by three days of prayers and fasting of the Jews, organized by her Uncle Mordecai, Esther defies tradition and initiates an audience with the King. This bold act is usually punishable by death. The King, however, is pleased to see her. And what does our Esther do? Instead of blurting out her pressing concern over the planned genocide of her people, she invites him to dinner.

> *Then the king asked, 'What is so urgent that you took your life in your hands to come to see me? What is your request? You may have anything you want, up to half the kingdom if you just ask.'* **(Esther 5:3, CWV)**

But Esther, unfazed by the offer of additional wealth and power, remains focussed and on-task.

> *If it pleases the king, I would like to invite you and Haman to be my guests at a special banquet I am preparing.* **(Esther 5:4, CWV)**

The king accepts the invitation, and during the festivities of the evening, again attempts to get to the root of Esther's concern. But, under Divine guidance, Esther bides her time and plans another more spectacular dinner.

> *If the king is so kind and willing to grant my request, I would like you and Haman to be my guests again the day after tomorrow, then I'll tell you both.* **(Esther 5:8, CWV)**

It is during the second dinner with King Ahasuerus and Haman that Esther unveils her own Jewish ancestry, relates the plight of her people and begs for the King's mercy. The King, furious when Esther reveals Haman as the architect of this wicked plan, leaves the room to gain his composure. He returns only to find Haman desperately begging the queen for forgiveness, and misinterprets the action for an attack on the Queen. Instantly, he commits him to death on the same gallows which Haman had earlier constructed for Esther's Uncle Mordecai, because he had refused to bow down to him. The King later commands Mordecai to override the first order of the killing of the Jews. The good news triggered two days of feasting and celebration. These days which mark the lifting of the King's order for the extinction of all Jews are still celebrated today in the Jewish holiday of *Purim* in late February or March. The primary imperative of this holiday is the reading or the hearing of the book of Esther. Esther's role in this drama remains as an example of the power of a woman who accepts her responsibility and assignment, understanding her place and position "for such a time as this."

References or sermons on these women of substance are few and far between. Instead, we hear of all of the Bible's vicious vixens: Jezebel, Potiphar's wife, Lot's wife, Delilah, Sapphira, to name a few. One cannot help but wonder of the heightened impact of the Church—internally and on civil society—if these Biblical examples of women of substance were widely disseminated. Would it result in greater numbers of women at decision-making, policy planning and implementation levels? Would paedophilia have been recognized, acknowledged and dealt with in the Roman Catholic Church before it could bring incalculable damage to countless families? Would the massive institutional cover-up have ensued? Would domestic violence and other gender-based discrimination be met with such stony silence from the Church? Rather than resisting and openly challenging external structures designed to keep women in subordinate roles, the contemporary Church, veering away from the path of the early Church, has bolstered these structures, using inaccurate Scriptural translations and interpretations to support their positions. This on-going battle between structure and substance mirrors that of the male disciples' preoccupation with placement and status against the primary concern of the women: ministering to Jesus up to His Death and Resurrection, and carrying out His work in preparation for His return.

This prioritizing of structure over substance has kept the Church outside, or at best, on the periphery of most social movements. The work of the Church in the Civil Rights and Anti-War Movement in the United States, the liberation theology in Latin America, and the role of the Christian Church in the anti-apartheid movement in South Africa are notable exceptions. For the most part, however, these struggles reflected the work of religious militants, progressive-thinking "renegade" sections of a larger body of Christ that frequently challenged their Christian activism. The front-runners of these progressive religious movements paid dearly for their social activism, bringing severe punishment and alienation of many. The preoccupation with structure over the substance of the message has left the Church exposed to internal and external vulnerabilities, primarily because the structure has bowed to the hierarchical models of the world. Hence it is difficult to argue against the perception of the Church as aligned to exploitative and oppressive structures, beginning with its inextricable ties to enslavement, colonialism, racism, male domination and gender discrimination and inequality. History remains a convincing witness. In fact organized religion continues to be dogged by the image of subordinating rather than supporting and promoting the development of women, both in their private and public roles. For these reasons, the Church has been seen as abrogating its transforming role for one that conforms to society. Thankfully, there are some exceptions in organizations such as Safe Haven Ministries, a U.S. organization that has been addressing domestic abuse from a Christian perspective since 1990.

This too-little-too-late response to urgent social issues is perhaps the primary reason for the growth of independent churches in response to the needs of an increasing demand for a more "touchy/feely" Christianity that relates to the specific needs of the grassroots and the poor, an overwhelming majority of whom, worldwide, are women. Interestingly, one of the main distinguishing features of these independent churches is the leadership roles of women, many of whom pastor their own churches. These independent churches or "small churches" as they are dubbed in the Caribbean, are characterized by a flexibility that allows them to employ direct-response strategies to deal with the poverty and other social ills that haunt low-income and socially vulnerable congregations. Unlike the structure-bound mainstream churches, they attempt a more grounded theology that unleashes a deeper understanding of faith and stresses a closer relationship with Jesus Christ for guidance in manoeuvering and overcoming day-to-day struggles. Their agenda of transformation often reaches beyond the impressive walls of the Church to challenge societal mores, attitudes and traditions. For the most part women are incorporated into the core of the ministries of these churches as part of their operating strategies. Their participation goes well beyond the predictable Women's Ministries, Mother's Day services—one-time tributes to women that fade with the passing of the moment—or children's stories, music ministry, preparation of meals or arranging of flowers, as important as these duties are.

The predominance of women in these independent Churches allows for a compassion and sensitivity that is drowned out in more structure-focussed churches. Women's presence and responsible power enable them to deal with the gender issues that are often lost or unrecognized in larger mainstream churches. It is here that issues such as gender-based violence, public and private work, incest, female economic dependence, female-headed households and feminized poverty reveal a link between the social, economic, political and religious that are not as readily addressed by mainstream churches. It calls for a faith, steeped in compassion and grounded in reality. Substance over structure.

Who can reach out to deal with these issues more than women?

> But the bridge between society and the church has been affected. The route through Christ has been affected. The Church is not as accessible to the world, and the world is not as accessible to Christ...hampered by the minimizing of women's roles.
>
> —Assistant Pastor Paula Olivier
> Seventh-day Adventist Church of the Oranges
> Orange, New Jersey

How has the furthering of the gospel suffered by this minimized participation of women? How many women who need the refreshing, saving grace of Jesus Christ have been turned away and alienated because they view Him through the messages sent by a male-dominated Church? More critically, how many well-meaning, activist women directly link women's continued oppression to repressive religious structures that ignore and tacitly condone the subjugation and discrimination of women? In a few cases, women have found ways of circumventing traditional structures to hold leadership roles in mainstream churches. The price, however, is high; the battle, on-going.

Perched atop a hill on the Loma Linda Campus in California is the Campus Hill Church, where Dr. Hyveth Williams is the senior pastor, the first Black female to pastor a Seventh-day Adventist Church. Hers is a Ministry that continues to be ensnared by its umbilical cord, even in the midst of its effectiveness, demand and proven track record. Attacks on her ministry continue, even in the midst of overwhelming success and worldwide acclamation. Slurs come through surface mail and electronic mail, the age of technology simply accelerating and making more effective and widespread blistering, well-orchestrated attacks that come from as far down under as Australia. At one point in an unending saga, there was a website designed specifically to attack this fearless woman of God. The prompt used: "If you have any dirt on Hyveth Williams, send it here."[27]

Ever seeking out the baseline truth, one of her main theories links women's destructive human relationships to a search for intimacy with men before they find it with God. She bases this on the Bible's frequent appeal for intimacy with God, an appeal that gets lost in the preoccupation with hierarchical structures, legalistic traditions, 'status mongering' egomania and the jostling for power that inhere in organized religion. Even as these men—not unlike the male disciples in Jesus' ministry—are consumed with earthly place in the religious kingdom that has been erroneously erected on earth, the body of Christ suffers. In contrast, women are consumed with pain, frustration, even terror, if they dare to answer the call of God to ministry.

The call for a deeper spiritual intimacy with God is one which women hear, understand and to which they respond, only if they are brave, stubborn and Divinely guided. In the attack on Pastor Williams, her detractors interpret her messages as a call to "sexual intimacy with God." This absurd interpretation, a classic example of the "Men are from Mars, Women are from Venus"[28] differences in communication and perspectives underscores the need, not only for women to minister to women, but for men to be exposed to the deeper and more vibrant understanding that women bring to a relationship with Jesus. More critically, it points to the failure of the Church to draw on the talents and skills of one sector of its population—a numerical majority at that—to meet the urgent needs that are beyond the understandings and abilities of

---

27   Personal communication with Dr. Hyveth Williams.
28   John Gray, *Men Are From Mars, Women Are From Venus: A Practical Guide for Improving and Getting What You Want in Relationships,* (New York: Harper Collins Publishers, 1992).

traditional preachers and teachers. The demand, then, is for a completely different perspective on the Bible and its application that could move the Church into a new dimension...for such a time as this. It is this new energy and perspective—a more feminized energy, if you will, that the Church sorely lacks.

According to Pastor Williams, men engage the Word from the outside, and do a tremendous job analyzing it hermeneutically. Women, however, step inside the text.

> We feel it; we sense it; we smell it; we taste it. We actually become the characters, and then we read out of it, before we can draw our lessons. And this is true of all women. This is why we need both, because one without the other gives a great imbalance.
>
> —Dr. Hyveth Williams
> Senior Pastor
> Campus Hill Church
> Loma Linda, California

It is an imbalance so closely linked to male domination that it enables the plight and concerns of women to fall on deaf ears, for the most part, as the Church assumes an ostrich-like, head-in-the-sand position. While this preaching from the "inside" has been derided as "womanist" preaching that unnecessarily whips up emotions, it has grabbed hold of the realities of women's lives, offering from the Word, solace, grace, comfort and understanding that speak to the unique brand of woman pain...a pain over which male religious leaders merely skim, if not miss habitually. More importantly, it provides a "womanist" perspective of hope and triumph, and a revelation of God's special place and grace for women in a way that no one had ever bothered to communicate to women. In more ways than one, it is an unveiling of God's feminine characteristics that have been so strategically down-played in the

Father God/Mother God duality from which our own image and likeness have been copied.

> ...the Bible tells us that God made us, both male and female, in His image. What we've presented traditionally is a God who is one-sided and only male. I've prayed to Father/Mother God. It is looked at with shock, and I wouldn't do it every day, but there have been times in my ministry that I have approached it from that. So people have been shocked, and I've received letters and things like that, so you have to be careful how you minister to and educate people. But the Bible does address God as Mother and as Father. But most people are not shocked because of the gender association, but mostly because it sounds so Roman Catholic.
>
> —Dr. Hyveth Williams
> Senior Pastor
> Campus Hill Church
> Loma Linda, California

Make no mistake about it, most men are intimidated by the concept of a Father/Mother God. Moreover, most Christian religions still tiptoe around the maternal characteristics of God. And to pray Father/Mother God unfortunately burps up unfounded associations with lesbianism or exaggerated Maryism. Deliberate or not, these are all elements of a persistent conspiracy that props up a patriarchal control that denies women and the substance they bring to Christianity. Yet it is precisely that compassion, tenderness and woman's touch that is required to combat the harsh focus on structure and its hierarchical preoccupations. Compassionate substance *versus* competitive structure.

On another hill hundreds of miles away in the Caribbean island of Barbados, Pastor Lucille Baird shepherds Mt. Zion Ministries, but experiences the challenges and obstacles that all women pastors face. She has been forced to contend with male imposition of Biblical patterns, texts and scriptures carefully interpreted to keep her in a place of silence, subordination and invisibility. Yet she remains adamant in her refusal to be "hemmed in," and "stereotyped."

> In Barbados, if a man is anointed and powerful and flowing with all the gifts, people say 'What a mighty man of God!' If a woman is similarly anointed, they say: 'What a Jezebel!' I've had to live with that, and break through that. Yes, an anointed woman of God, because you speak with authority, and you speak with power. Authority and power are considered too manly. That's for the man, that's not your role (so they think). You should sit and be quiet. Go home and sit and learn in silence.
>
> —Pastor Lucille Baird
> Mt. Zion Ministries
> Barbados, W.I.

The Church has indeed paid a high cost for this imposed silence of women and the consequent submergence of its female characteristics. More specifically, it has robbed itself of the gifts that are uniquely attributed to women, diminishing its power in the lives of women and men.

> Everything is filtered through a male-dominated world-view. We don't exercise the same confidence in women that Christ had on the women in His Ministry. Women were, in the mind of Jesus, meant to play a greater role in the church than they are allowed to play in the contemporary Church.
>
> —Pastor Paula Fils-Aime
> Miami, Florida

Ironically, many women feel that women themselves are responsible for the solution. Even though this response resembles the classic "blame the victim" syndrome, it holds as critical the need to carefully consider the power which women themselves possess to address and change the situation.

> Women that allow men, or any particular system to hem them in are their own obstacles, or have put obstacles in their own way. They don't have to take it. And I think, unfortunately, some of the women too don't really know who they are, because the teaching that the forefathers has imparted to the older Church, (the Church years ago, and even sometimes today in the present Church) has caused women to be dormant and passive and laid back and complacent. I think that we need to look at the way we teach women.
>
> —Pastor Lucille Baird
> Mt. Zion Ministries
> Barbados, W.I.

Indeed the urging of women to excavate their true selves from within The Word and beneath the interpretations that deliberately craft their subordination and inaction holds the key to the true liberation of a Church held hostage by worldly hierarchical traditions. Even in the independent churches with progressive world views that permit leadership roles for women in the way that the traditional churches still do not, there are women, unfamiliar with their true roles, who take issue with women religious leaders. This is not shocking, since at the core of any oppressive agenda is the targeting of the oppressed to sign on, agree, cooperate and collaborate in their own oppression.

> And the women would want to impose what they think or perceive that their role should be on other women to make them 'behave' and 'fall in line', and so women would do that. I think they're well-intentioned, I don't think they mean any malice, really. I think they've been indoctrinated, and they think that's it, and they want to be what the stereotyped women should be. But look at

the Bible. All through the Bible I see very powerful women. I don't see any weak women at all in the Bible. **I want to be who God wants me to be.**

—Pastor Lucille Baird
Barbados, W.I.

A major task then is the re-education of women to their own empowered role and function, and its strategic, Esther-like importance for such a time as this. First of all, there is the need to widely disseminate an awareness of Jesus' radical action in calling women to be disciples.

And it is important for people to understand that Jesus did call women to be His disciples. People don't understand this because the writers, under the inspiration of the Holy Spirit, did not see women's issues as a priority. They saw Salvation as the priority, because they themselves had come to the conclusion, in the words of the Apostle Paul, that when you accept Jesus Christ as your personal Saviour, all of the humanly constructed barriers and prejudices come tumbling down. So that rather than make women the issue, they made Salvation the issue, knowing that if you're saved, you overcome those prejudices. The Church became so watered down with socio-political agendae that they lost track of this truth.

—Dr. Hyveth Williams
Senior Pastor Campus Hill Church
Loma Linda, California

Indeed in his letter to the Church in Corinth, Paul reminded them that those in Christ are new creatures.

Therefore, if any man be in Christ, he is a new creature; Old things are passed away; behold, all things are become new. **(Corinthinans 5:17, KJV)**

And lest we think that the world's hierarchical structures were not included in these "old things" that were wiped away through Christ's saving grace, Paul breaks it down in his letter to the Galatians.

> *For as many of you as have been baptized into Christ have put on Christ. There is neither Jew nor Greek, there is neither bond nor free, there is neither male nor female: for ye are all one in Christ Jesus.*
> *(Galatians 3:27-28, KJV)*

It is a critical text that speaks to the banishing of all inequities, inequalities and distinctions, and the full incorporation of all believers into God's family, "with all the attendant rights and privileges," according to the notes of the NIV translation. Moreover, again referencing the NIV notes, "Unity in Christ transcends ethnic, social and sexual distinctions."[29] Attendant rights and privileges carry tremendous responsibilities: the responsibility for women, as daughters of Abraham, to take hold of the promises of God and use all skills, talents and resources to disseminate the good news of His Saving Grace in the same way that men do; the responsibility for men to assist, not attack; support, not sabotage; collaborate, not contest the work of women. Salvation is indeed the issue; and wordly, male-dominant ideas, ideologies, scriptural misinterpretations and their accompanying strategies and man-made laws to keep women from actively participating in the Salvation agenda are un-Biblical and divisive, revealing the hand of evil, destructive and un-Godly forces.

Sadly, the prioritizing of socio-political concerns over Biblical truth—without linking both—has forced the Church to succumb to worldly dictates and societal patterns that have compromised its mandate and backed it

---

29   Kenneth Barker, "Galatians 3:28," *The NIV Study Bible* (Grand Rapids, Michigan: Zondervan Publishing House, 1985), 1785.

into a role of follower rather than leader. The Church then finds itself as a chief agent in maintaining a *status quo* that includes the subordination of women. Moreover, this subordination is linked to the violence of women and children. This is occurring at a period in world history when one in every three women has been beaten, coerced into sex or otherwise abused in her lifetime. Frequently the abuser is a member of her own family, often with deep-rooted religious affiliations.

Some gains are being made in a few churches—especially the independent churches— to break away from a **follow-ship** position in order to retrieve and re-establish their leadership roles, and engender true **fellowship**. However, the traditional churches totter in efforts to stay relevant…and to hold on to their congregations. Attempts to prepare and direct women into leadership roles conflict with traditional attitudes on restricting women from performing important ceremonies such as marriages, baptisms, and from becoming fully ordained ministers. Symbolic support of women leaders contradicts the quick withdrawal of that support when women ministers are attacked, harassed, intimidated or attempts made to discredit them. For example, women ministers, who are more vulnerable to spurious charges because of the resentment of their leadership roles, very rarely enjoy the full support and protection from large religious bodies that men readily receive, even when they are proven in error. The seemingly deliberate, strategic, persistent and unrepentant cover-up of the Roman Catholic Church and its protection of erring priests, in the glare of untold damage to children and young men, reflect a privilege of protection that remains the prerogative of male religious leaders. Again, the task falls, perhaps unfairly, on women, as the moral and numerical majority of the Church, to help steer it back on course. It is a task that is difficult to fulfil when the true role, purpose and function of women are still clouded in misinterpretations, mis-perceptions and hidden truths.

The horror of operating in an environment—influenced by a world hierarchical system— which forces the questioning of God's call on one's life is constantly faced by women of God. The horror goes beyond women's personal struggles and spiritual development to their external link and impact on the world around them. How have women's arrested spiritual development within the Church negatively impacted the development of women overall, and by extension, the development of society to which it is so directly tied? How have the Church and society been robbed of the spiritual substance of women? How has the preoccupation with structure, which pervades Christianity, restricted the growth of the gospel and put at risk the lives of women and children? The critical and yet-to-be-fully-explored-and-addressed link between women in the Church and women's poverty, discrimination and inequality is central to development processes that focus on the economic and political empowerment of women.

For example, Christian Aid is an international development organization that operates in over 60 of the world's poorest countries. It is an agency of 40 British and Irish 'sponsoring churches' working, wherever the need is, irrespective of religion, and supporting local organizations, which are best placed to understand local needs. This Christian-based organization believes in strengthening people to find their own solutions to the problems they face, while striving for a new world transformed by an end to poverty. In addition, it campaigns to change the rules that keep people poor. It is no surprise then, that this organization addresses the empowerment of women as a core development strategy. How pervasive are these concepts and linkages of spirituality and development within the body of Christ? The most burdensome element in this discussion are the ramifications of a misunderstood Christ in a development movement which mirrors His empathy and concern for the impoverished, the dispossessed and the oppressed. More critically, it is a movement which recognizes the need of a Divine force, but treats with studied cynicism the malecentric, male-dominated religions and their egocentric representatives. Understandably.

Indeed there is need for a more *genderstood* look at the Life and Ministry of Jesus; His appreciation of women, and the way in which He valued, respected, honoured, defended and promoted their interests. The way in which the New Testament women utilized their experience with Christ becomes a measure for understanding, not only the degree to which He treasured, trusted and valued them, but the degree to which He honoured women by including them in His Resurrection. This perception underscores a lopsided contemporary Christian agenda that does not sufficiently integrate and include the unique understandings, perceptions and contributions of women. It is important to repeat this indisputable fact: The women believed Jesus' constant references to His Death and Resurrection. They took Him at His Word, and prepared accordingly. The men allowed their own worldly, hierarchical self-interest and status-seeking to preoccupy their minds. Moreover, they could not bring themselves to believe the women. How relevant are these lessons for the contemporary Church? What is the nature and essence of the substance being minimized and marginalized for a structure that keeps its Godly mission in perpetual danger? How has the Christian Church been affected by this persistent inability to emulate and pass on Jesus' perception and appreciation of women?

> I think they still don't get it. The majority of men, when I talk to them one on one, they love their wives. But they

see them as support, not equals. They see them as good women who support them, help them get to the top, and they look after them and bring them along and make them eat from the same table, though they may sit at the foot of it. It has been affected in a very destructive way, because, in my opinion, the Christian Church has given a warped image of God by not accessing the availability of women.

—Dr. Hyveth Williams
Associate Pastor
Campus Hill Church
Loma Linda, California

Jesus certainly accessed these women of substance at the foot of the cross, who became major players at the transition of His ministry. More importantly, He allowed them easy access to Him. The reluctance of the Church to expose women to this truth and to facilitate women in understanding and assuming—without harassment—their unique place and space continues to be a grave danger not only for women, but for the Church and the entire human society.

Genderstanding Jesus:
Questions for Reflection, Discussion and Action
Chapter 6

1). Has the spread of the gospel suffered from the minimized participation of women?

2). Does the Church condone the subjugation and discrimination of women?

3). How is the substance of the Gospel being overshadowed by the structure of the Church?

4). What is the work—individual and collective—that you have been called to do? What is your Ministry?

5). What do you need to work that Work?

6). What are the obstacles, perceived, existing or imaginary, to working your Work?

7). What strategies have you designed to circumvent these obstacles?

8). Design a strategic Work Plan for your Ministry.

Chapter 7

"WOMEN, WHY WEEPEST THOU?"

It occurred to me one late summer Sunday evening that Jesus was minding my business. Not only was He minding my business, He was intimately involved in the tiniest details. We had just driven from New York, the four-hour ride stretching to over five hours because of the Sunday evening exodus from the Big Apple. My husband was tired from driving and hungry. I was tired from being driven, and the thought of having to cook. Neither of us wanted to stop to pick up something to eat. I was concentrating more on not letting the fact that I had to cook put me in bad humour than the bare fact that there was nothing to cook. I opened the refrigerator, and there, neatly packaged, was a dish of fresh green string beans, with the ends already carefully clipped and the string pulled off the side, begging for a pot in which to simmer. They had been too much for the dish I had prepared for the repast of a deceased Church sister. I had packed them to take to my sister in New York, but had forgotten them. Jesus had been in my business then.

A peep in the freezer turned up a package of cooked rice. My intention then had been to cook two cups of rice, but preoccupied, I had measured four cups of rice, and discovered the error at the very moment the last grain hit the pot of boiling water. So I had carefully frozen half of the cooked rice for a time such as this. He was in my business that day too. Before I could even think, as if on automatic, I had pounded some fresh garlic, added it to the hot oil in

129

the pot, added my paste of fresh curry powder and water, and in no time at all the string beans were getting happy in curry and lemon pepper. I discovered a prized can of garbanzo (chick) peas and added those to the mix. Meanwhile, my rice was making merry in the microwave. We had long discussed our intentions to become vegetarians, and that would provide the argument against any comments about missing meat protein. The discovery of a fresh pack of pre-washed salad, washed again for security, completed the meal. Jesus was all up in my business that Sunday evening, concerned about my need to create a good meal out of nothing, in the same way He was concerned about wine[30] running out in the middle of the wedding fete that day in Canaan. It is the same Jesus, concerned about the pain women suffer both inside and outside of religious organizations, who asks:

Women, why weepest thou?   *(John 20:15, KJV)*

It was the first question He asked after His Resurrection. The women: Mary, the Mother of Jesus, Mary, the wife of Cleophas, Mary Magdalene, Martha, Joanna, Susanna and others who were spiritually developed and prepared were there, spices in hand, ready for any eventuality. Having discovered the empty grave, they ran back to inform the brothers, who were locked up in a room, afraid of the possibility of being subjected to the same fate that their Lord had suffered. Obviously, they still hadn't gotten it! It is perhaps here that the urgent need for gender balance, inclusion and male/female collaboration are most

---

30   This is as good a place as any to voice my own horror at revisionary interpretations that suggest the miracle turned water into "grape juice" or "punch" instead of wine. After all, how much more miraculous is turning water into good wine than punch or grape juice? These are the same forces that diminish women's participation and contribution to His Ministry in some misguided effort to fit man-made religious and socio-political guidelines.

dramatically displayed. Jesus emphasizes and ensures prime participation by women through His first appearance to the women who had followed Him to the foot of the cross, remained and returned to His grave. But He is even more specific and direct in His emphasis:

Whom seekest thou?   *(John 20:15, KJV)*

He asks. He knew they were looking for Him, but the question implies a constant reminder that He must always be the object of our search. The moment we women and men shift our gaze from Him, we leave ourselves vulnerable to man-made systems, structures and traditions that are directly opposed to His all-inclusive Message and Ministry. It is a cautionary note for women as well as men, for individuals as well as the corporate body. For even as women struggle against the tide of oppressive, male-exclusive structures, it is only a studied focus on Him as the object of our search that will heal the hurts, the scars and the resentment that could bring about spiritual suicide. A most powerful and inspiring message comes via cyberspace, titled: "A Carrot; An Egg; or A Cup of Coffe."

A young woman went to her mother and told her about her life and how things were so hard for her. She did not know how she was going to make it and wanted to give up. She was tired of fighting and struggling. It seemed as one problem was solved a new one arose. Her mother took her to the kitchen, filled three pots with water and placed each on a high fire. Soon the pots came to a boil. In the first, she placed carrots, in the second she placed eggs, and the last she placed ground coffee beans. She let them sit and boil, without saying a word. In about twenty minutes she turned off the burners. She fished the carrots out and placed them in a bowl. She pulled the eggs out and placed them in a bowl. Then she ladled the coffee out and placed it in a bowl. Turning to her daughter, she asked, Tell me, what do you see? Carrots, eggs, and coffee, she replied.

She brought her closer and asked her to feel the carrots. She did and noted that they were soft.

She then asked her to take an egg and break it. After pulling off the shell, she observed the hard-boiled egg. Finally, she asked her to sip the coffee. The daughter smiled, as she tasted its rich aroma. The daughter then asked. What does it mean, mother?

Her mother explained that each of these objects had faced the same adversity—boiling water—but each reacted differently.

The carrot went in strong, hard, and unrelenting. However, after being subjected to the boiling water, it softened and became weak. The egg had been fragile. Its thin outer shell had protected its liquid interior. But, after sitting through the boiling water, its inside became hardened.

The ground coffee beans were unique, however. After they were in the boiling water, they had changed the water.

Which are you? she asked her daughter. When adversity knocks on your door, how do you respond? Are you a carrot, an egg, or a coffee bean?

Think of this: Which am I? Am I the carrot that seems strong, but with pain and adversity, do I wilt and become soft and lose my strength?

Am I the egg that starts with a malleable heart, but changes with the heat? Did I have a fluid spirit, but after a death, a breakup, a financial hardship or gender discrimination or some other trial, have I become hardened and stiff? Does my shell look the same, but on the inside am I bitter and tough with a stiff spirit and hardened heart?

Or, am I like the coffee bean? The bean actually changes the hot water, the very circumstance that brings the pain. When the water gets hot, it releases the fragrance and flavor. If you are like the bean, when things are at their worst, you get better and change the situation around you. When the hour is the darkest, and trials are their greatest do you elevate to another level? How do you handle adversity? Are you a carrot, an egg, or a coffee bean? Count your blessings, not your problems.

This story begs the question: how do we handle gender discrimination? Will we wilt and become soft? Will we allow the heat to harden our hearts, making us disgruntled, distrustful and discouraged? Or, will the ideas and issues explored in the last chapters bring us to a *genderstanding* of Jesus that will strengthen us to become the fragrance filled and flavourful beans that we have been charged to be? *Become a Beanie!*

So while the tears clean the cobwebs from our eyes, our gaze must remain fixed, our hopes bright, our vision focused on Him, His Mission, and the plan and purpose to which He has called us. It is about Kingdom-building, not king-making or queen-making. It is about Him, not him or her, with as much focus on The Caller as on "The Call." This purpose-focused approach can only come and, more critically, be maintained by a stubborn connection to God…Father, Son and Holy Spirit. When our church or our religion seems at odds with this purpose-focus, it is time for us to remember His question: *"Whom Seekest Thou?"* It is time to get busy about releasing our fragrance and flavour into the heat of gender-related adversity.

God has long before promised that if we seek Him, we will find Him. This promise applies every bit to women as to men. So it is in finding Him that we will become confident and adamant about His answer to our call, as we respond to His call on our lives. More often than not it is a call to get real with Jesus. Often accompanying a truthful acknowledgment of this reality is an understanding of the boulders, boundaries and barriers that beset us as we attempt to go about His business. They come in self-doubt and second-guessing. They come in criticism from others, women as well as men. They take the form of intimidation of the task to which we are called. Can I do this? Am I capable? How would the Church Board respond? Am I the first woman to do this? Will I be stepping out of my assigned role as a woman? Lord, are You sure You want

<u>me</u> to do this? Are you sure you have the right person, Lord? What about Brother Alfred, surely he could do a better job? And Lord, you know these men can't deal with women as leaders. Lord, am I trained to do this work?

When Mary continued to question Him about the whereabouts of her Saviour's body, Jesus called her by name: **"Mary,"**…and she instantly recognized His Voice. How do we women respond when He calls <u>our</u> name? Do we recognize His Voice? Do we have the time to listen? Do we **make** the time to listen? Do we respond immediately, or are we too cowed by man-made traditions? Are we too comfortable in our carefully contrived cocoons that we remain immobile and immobilized?

Then there are the excuses: Too busy; too shy; too poor; not enough education; not enough training; not enough music lessons. Can't speak; can't write; can't preach; can't sing; can't count; can't organize; can't lead; can't upstage my mate. These are all mind games designed to keep us in background roles. They point to the degree to which women have subconsciously collaborated with their own subjugation. But one thing we are sure about is that God does not necessarily call the qualified. What He is faithful in doing, however, is qualifying the called, seeking first the requirements of willing and available spirits. The woman at the well got a crash course in His messianic agenda, before departing on her mission of spreading the good news and winning souls in the village. Mary, the sister of Martha vacated her kitchen duty to be trained at His feet for more active duty at His Crucifixion and Resurrection. Martha, the perfect hostess, and one with an impressive serving of spiritual maturity and understanding, used both her spiritual gifts and gift of hospitality as Bishop of one of the early churches. He has been consistent about confirming His Call, and supporting His called. The Bible is replete with such examples: Mary, at the birth of Jesus, receiving confirmation from cousin Elizabeth and support from husband Joseph. Saul, blinded on the road to Damascus, receives confirmation through the sudden return of his vision, when Ananias visited and laid hands on him, and "something like scales fell from Saul's eyes, and he could see again." (*Acts 9:18, NIV*). Sometimes the Lord can be dramatically literal.

And then there is that ugly four letter word: F-E-A-R. Save us, Lord! We can glibly cite all of the faith-filled passages in the Bible, and that's terrific. But when the rubber meets the road, it robs us of our courage and spirit, if we're not battle-ready. When we women are called to be pioneers for Him, do we stand firm, or crumble like one of our most delicious home-baked cookies? How has fear prevented us from hearing, listening, and acting on the specific tasks for which God has targeted us and prepared us? These tasks may or may not be starring in leadership positions, but they certainly have not been restricted to back-up singing roles. Honourable and important as these duties are, all women have not been called exclusively to sweep churches, prepare meals, dust pastors' desks, arrange flowers and narrate children's stories. The women in the Bible who broke through barriers, defied traditional boundaries and went beyond constricting spaces, doing so because they kept their gaze on Jesus. They focused on Him, and remained connected. The onus is on us to know who we are in the Lord. *Stay connected!*

Women today are blessed to be living in an age where we have direct access to God's Word. We can read the Bible for ourselves and depend on the Holy Spirit to interpret its meaning and application in our lives. This is not a freedom to be taken lightly. It is only in recent history that the Roman Catholic Church, for example, allows its followers to read the Bible for themselves. In some countries, Christian women and men can still be imprisoned and killed for even owning a Bible. While the increasing literacy of women permits personal reading, the tradition of being fed diluted, watered down, inaccurately interpreted scriptures has played a big part in the spiritual stifling that most women experience. Given the powerful messages and examples of involved women in the Bible, it is incumbent on every literate woman to read, explore and seek understanding of The Word for herself. It is more critical to become familiar with scriptures which have been skillfully employed to undermine and minimize women's participation and contribution to the spreading of the Gospel, and to understand the context in which these scriptures were used, in order to challenge their inappropriate application to the contemporary Church.

Conversely, it is even *more* critical to excavate scriptures that empower women. Moreover, it is important to use every medium within women's vast creative and resourceful repertoire to share, discuss and disseminate our own findings and revelations. Lunches, brunches, tea parties, book clubs, garden clubs, manicure parties, Avon and Tupper Ware parties, bridal showers, make-up parties, recipe clubs, women's ministries and other women-focused gatherings represent opportunities for sharing women's Biblical truth. Staying in The Word is the only route to staying connected. As one female pastor confidently announced: "I am who the Word says I am." But it is only constant studying of the Word that can bring about this knowledge and confidence. *Stay in The Word!*

Vigilance is a word that appears to come to mind only when we are protecting our husbands or our children. The same energy and attention must be given to efforts to distract and detract women from realizing their full Godly potential. There is no doubt in my mind that the plot to ignore, minimize, devalue or discourage the contributions of women in the contemporary Christian Church is exactly that…a plot of the enemy. The pastor with whom I argued, as narrated at the beginning of this work, was in the right area, but the wrong street. It is not feminism that is evil, as he perceives it, but the structural divisions that have caused, concretized and institutionalized women's subordinate positions and imbued them with a sense of normalcy. Therein lies the evil. Women must assume the responsibility of keeping themselves informed in order to protect their interests and defend their human rights. Moreover, we must assume the responsibility of passing on new knowledge and understanding to other Christian women and men, particularly younger women and men. The responsibility of socializing our children falls mainly on women, and herein lies the greatest power for re-education and for transforming attitudes. We must also be aware of the ease with which hard-earned rights can be chiseled away and reversed, if not protected and defended. *Stay vigilant!*

It never ceases to amaze me how uneasy most men—and more women than we care to acknowledge—become around the subject of women's equality, empowerment or rights. The word "feminism" is often a flag for all-out war and requires a particular sensitivity in explaining. In 1895, the word "feminism" was described as a woman who has in her the capacity of fighting her way back to independence. As far back as 1913, a feminist activist, Rebecca West wrote: "I myself never have been able to find out precisely what feminism is. I only know that people call me a feminist whenever I express sentiments that differentiate me from a doormat."[31] These misunderstandings are pregnant with opportunities for discussions and platforms for informed debates that could only facilitate the easing of tensions as they broaden and deepen awareness of problems that will re-emerge when swept under the mat. Admittedly there are hard truths which both women and men might find difficult to grasp. It is as difficult to bring men to the understanding of the ways—covert and overt, subconscious and conscious— in

---

31   Rebecca West, "The Clarion," 14 Nov. 1913.

which they disrespect, humiliate, alienate and subordinate women, as it is to convey to women the ways in which we are socializing boys to continue this behaviour, and girls to accept it. Moreover, many women, unfulfilled and forced to stymie our own dreams, can be resentful and unsupportive of women who break through barriers and restrictions that were heretofore taken for granted.

Ironically, in avoiding or rejecting supportive friendships of other women, women are not tapping in to the very experience that could be most healing. Scientists at UCLA and Penn State University have discovered that women have different and/or additional stress-fighting mechanisms than the "fight or flight" mechanism that has been discovered in research conducted on men. According to Dr. Laura Cousin Klein, Assistant Professor of Biobehavioral Health at Penn State University:

> ...it seems that when the hormone oxytocin is released as part of the stress responses in a woman, it buffers the fight or flight response and encourages her to tend children and gather with other women instead. When she actually engages in this tending or befriending, studies suggest that more oxytocin is released, which further counters stress and produces a calming effect.

> ...The fact that women respond to stress differently than men has significant implications for our health. It may take some time for new studies to reveal all the ways that oxytocin encourages us to care for children and hang out with other women, but the "tend and befriend" notion developed by Drs. Klein and Taylor may explain why women consistently outlive men...

This need to "tend and befriend" in the face of on-going stress may well be the reason that women instinctively hold tea parties, bridal and birth showers and other feminine-focused opportunities to bond and share information. The general feeling, however, is that women tend not to prioritize or attach enough importance and attention to these relationships and opportunities in the way that men do. How many single women complain that their friendships become a casualty when one gets married?

> …Yet, if friends counter the stress that seems to swallow up so much of our life these days, if they keep us healthy and even add years to our life, why is it so hard to find time to be with them? That's a question that also troubles researcher, Ruthellen Josselson, Ph. D., co-author of *Best Friends: The Pleasures and Perils of Girls' and Women's Friendships*.[32] Every time we get overly busy with work and family, the first thing we do is let go of friendships with other women, explains Dr. Josselson. We push them right to the back burner. That's really a mistake because women are such a source of strength to each other. We nurture one another. And we need to have unpressured space in which we can do the special kind of talk that women do when they're with other women. It's a very healing experience.

Could this then be the reason that, under stress from the experience of witnessing the Crucifixion, the women who followed Jesus immediately went into the "tend and befriend" mode, ministering to Him and bonding with each other, while the men automatically went into the "fight or flight" mode? Is the Church ignoring opportunities to more strategically integrate and employ women's "tend and befriend" tendencies in Church policies and plans, particularly in this peculiar period in world history? There is need for much prayer about this entire subject of gender relations in the Church. For as the Church is beginning—all too slowly—to re-evaluate its position on women and attempt changes— some superficial, some substantial— it must assume the additional responsibility of preparing congregations, both men and women, for accepting and supporting women in untraditional roles. It

---

32   Three Rivers Press, 1998.

is critical to understand how deeply traditions and prejudices run, cutting as sharply in gender as in issues of race. Education, information, and constant exposure to healthy discussions on the subject are required in order to establish new guidelines for absorbing the transforming message of the gospel. Women, as well as men, can be intimidated by the new understandings and urgings under the Holy Spirit, and it is here that we must pay close attention and apply every sensitivity, reminded of His promise to do a new thing in us (*Isaiah 43:19*). Women and men who are led by the Spirit to engage this particular challenge, must take heed of the Biblical direction to be wise as a serpent but harmless as a dove. *Wise up!*

At the core of wisdom, however, is obedience. Obedience is the key to staying connected and gaining wisdom and direction from that connection. The direction often leads to the chiseling away of unwanted areas as we are sharpened and readied for more pointed action. This obedience demands that women follow God's leading and answer the call on our lives, in spite of existing and newly-constructed obstacles. It demands too that men be obedient to God's direction in confronting and tearing down worldly structures that create divisions in the Body of Christ and block the participation and contribution of all of its people. Christ's ministry on earth has presented a model of humility, not arrogance and egotism; of inclusion, not exclusion and elitism; of the strategic importance of collaboration, not competition; of the inclusion and promotion of women, not of the subjugation and domination of women and confinement to subordinate roles; of keeping our eyes upwards on the Father for spiritual guidance, not downwards on earthly man-made structures designed to rule, control, dominate and divide, and more critically, contradict His Will and Design. *Stay Obedient!*

Perhaps the most significant characteristic of Jesus Christ was His compassion...the compassion that triggered His selection of the woman at the well to lead out in announcing His Mission; the compassion that caused Him to pause, draw out and heal the woman with the issue of blood, in full knowledge that He was defying cultural traditions; the same compassion that motivated Him to acknowledge, appreciate and honour Mary Magdalene as she violated rules of propriety to "storm"[33] an exclusive dinner party to anoint Him for burial. His understanding of the challenges women would face in attempting to carry out His work prompted Him to proclaim the need to broadcast Mary's anointing of His feet, not for the act itself, but for the depth of understanding, belief and spiritual readiness that must be emulated. *Stay Prepared!*

The compassion of women has long been celebrated as though it is an innate characteristic of womanhood. While this may not be scientifically proven, women, because of our nurturing role tend indeed to be more compassionate. It is a characteristic that must be highly valued, honed, guarded and emulated, particularly as women struggle for and win some semblance of equality. Many women complain that women often lose this compassion, sensitivity and tenderness as they attain the rare heights of social, economic and professional ladders and break through glass ceilings. It is this compassion, however, that catapults us to greater spiritual heights. Rather than assuming that women in leadership positions automatically possess Jezebel spirits, we must actively seek ways in which we can support women in positions of power, exercising tremendous compassion and understanding of the internal and external struggles they face. Too often we become self-righteous judge and jury as we quickly

---

33   A colloquial expression from Trinidad and Tobago that means to gain admission, either without paying the required admission charge, or without being invited.

condemn women, without granting to them the kinds of allowances and benefit of the doubt that we so readily give to men. Unfortunately, men have no monopoly of this tendency. Compassion is often overshadowed by competition; collaboration and cooperation falling prey to contestation; and yes, empathy outweighed by envy.

Resolution calls for a deep understanding that women, whether perceived as powerful or powerless, are prisoners of a vicious system of structured inequality that pits us against each other, with the sole purpose of keeping both, the powerful and powerless, in supposedly pre-ordained positions. For example, the most visible and courageous women activists are often perceived as the deadly enemies of the very women on whose behalf they agitate. Such is the power of the internalised oppression to which all women have been subjected. The strategies employed against each other can be subtle, or blatant. Shunning, gossiping, rumour-mongering and jealousy are all part of a deadly arsenal of weapons of sisterhood destruction. Single women are often even more victimized by other women, leaving the role of single female pastors an often unenviable challenge.

In her book "Woman's Inhumanity to Woman," Phyllis Chesler addresses the frequent needs of women to take out their frustrations on each other, suggesting that even as we examine women's inequality and its source of male domination, we must, in the essence of fairness, keeping it real, and the quest for solutions, examine the ways in which women contribute to the pain, frustration and agony of other women. According to Chesler, "the situation is complicated by unspoken, unacknowledged, psychologically internalized double and triple gender standards." Moreover, she continues, "women's expectations of each other at work are often unrealistic, sexist, and characterized by unspoken ambivalence, regardless of who objectively holds more power."

It is not my intention to "blame the victim," by blaming women for the often negative ways in which we respond to our own second-class citizenship. However, we need to be reminded that the structures of domination and subordination have been imposed on both women and men, and women have been brainwashed into a place of subjectivity. There is, then, an urgent need to focus on our peculiar vulnerabilities, be vigilant in guarding against them and, with compassion and understanding, devise strategies to navigate around them.

I recall an incident during the writing of this chapter, while attending a funeral in Trinidad, the larger of the two-island country of Trinidad and Tobago, W. I. Having arrived just as the funeral had begun, I stood at the door, trying to plot the least disruptive entry into the packed congregation. Unfortunately, the pews on the side of the church on which I was standing were completely filled. I would have to cross the centre aisle to get over to the other side of the church. The door at which I was standing led directly into the cross aisle to get me over to the other side. However, the only problem was that the door and the cross aisle were very near to the front of the church. I looked around and inquired about church protocol from the first person I saw who seemed familiar with the church. He assured me that I could cross the aisle as soon as the speakers had finished.

Timing my entrance carefully to hurry to the seat during the exchanging of speakers, I scooted across the aisle. Just as I reached safely on the other side (so I thought) a woman beckoned to me. She looked familiar, and I thought she was motioning me to the empty seats next to her, so I sat down, foregoing the vacant spaces farther across to which I had been making my way. "You shouldn't walk across the aisle like that," she whispered viciously. My surprise did not get the better of me. "Didn't you see me carefully wait until the speakers were finished speaking?" I whispered back in the most imperial tone I could muster. She began her retort: "Well in this church they don't like you to…" "Excuse me," came my now icy tone, manicured index finger in full point position… "I want to listen to the speaker." "Well do that!" she bested me on ice. I still can't get over the shock of walking right into an unexpected cat-fight in the middle of God's house. Nearing the end of the service, after I had "borrowed" the service programme from the woman on my right (Sister Church-Seating Police was sitting on my left) and after some loud Hallelujahs from me, perhaps more in a Pharisaical show that I was absorbed in the service and unruffled by her undeserved aggression, (mercy, Lord!) my temptress handed me one of the three programmes she had been clutching to her bosom. By this time the Lord had filled me with a peace that certainly passed my own understanding of why I had dropped the incident at the end of the service.

But the enemy was not finished with us! Two days later, I was greeting a friend at church, and saw the same woman, in the company of my friend. "Were you the woman who was so rude to me at the funeral?" "Yes," she responded quietly. "You owe me an apology,' I demanded. "Yes," she said quietly, but made no move to offer the demanded apology. "That is no way for Christians to treat each other," I persisted, as though my own behaviour represented the model of Christian compassion and turning the other cheek. "Yes," she agreed. The Holy Spirit tied my tongue after that, but my friend gave me the "skinny" later. Apparently the woman was disturbed, not by my crossing the aisle once the service had begun, but "the pomp, circumstance and show," with which she accused me of entering the church. Well, forgive me for breathing!…although I have to confess that I was wearing a drop-dead black and white hat. She also took issue with my "short dress," even though my simple mid-calf black dress was well below the knees.

This incident is a perfect example of the pettiness with which we women can occupy ourselves, and the indirect rather than direct aggression which Chesler observed women usually use to attack each other. They are relationships devoid of the compassion that Jesus recognized in the women in His Ministry, and which He rewarded with such honour, tribute and deliverance. As I searched for the Divine lesson that was intended for me in that experience, I was convicted in a sermon by Pastor Annette Taylor: "Even when we are not responsible, our response can make the difference." Ouch! She was not finished with me yet. "We need to recognize the voice of the enemy, and guard our hearts with all diligence." More blows! And then, the stinging *coup de grace*: "Jesus came to perfect relationships. <u>Compassion</u> is the antidote to the bitterness in relationships."[34] Sadly, my own response had been anything but compassionate.

Compassion, like the true Christianity it denotes, cannot be parked some place when we're ready to *deal* with someone or some issue. And I do mean *DEAL*! Years ago in the early days of my renewed Christian experience, I struggled at work with managing an extremely difficult female assistant, whom I myself had hired. Caribbean grand-mothers call that "cutting a whip to beat yuh own tail!" And as I sought for a Christian response to her laziness, insensitivity and blatant insubordination, my thoughts fell on those old, heavy irons that were used to iron clothes in days that are thankfully far behind us. They would be placed on coal-pots filled with red hot coals, removed when scorching hot, and placed on wrinkled sheets and shirts that didn't dare resist their weight and heat. I owned a small collection of those antique irons, so I took one to my office and placed it on my desk as a paperweight. Its function was far more important, however. It

---

34   Thanks to Pastor Annette Taylor of Bethel Outreach Ministries for administering this well-deserved rod of correction.

was a secret reminder of the new brand which had been seared on me to remove every wrinkle, spot or stain, and which I was expected to advertise and promote **at all times**. It was not an easy struggle. In fact it is a continuing struggle, as we are continuously challenged by the forces around us. *Stay Compassionate!*

Note that *passion* is the root word of the all-important *compassion*. Instead of the petty rivalry for which women have been too often maligned, the women who ministered to Jesus throughout His Ministry were filled with a passion that overcame the fear of criticism, that challenged traditions and that permitted them to block out earthly symbols of success and examples of past failings to grasp His word and His promises. The same passion that came over the Samaritan woman at the well, compelling her to broadcast the news of the presence of the Messiah to the men in her village, strengthened Mary's resolve to crash Simon's fancy dinner party to anoint her Saviour's Feet. The very same passion operated to embolden the women to remain at the foot of the cross. It was passion for their Saviour and His Message that fueled their courage to seek His Body, to discover the empty tomb, and to be rewarded with an eye-witness news account of His Resurrection. Indeed one can argue that it is women's passion that has been marginalized and sidelined along with their participation at leadership levels, leaving a crisp, desiccated message that is thirsty for the juices of women's passion, purpose and the pregnant pain that brings new birth. It has left in its wake a skeleton body of Christ that hungers for the flesh of balance, true caring, and passionate concern and involvement in the lives of its congregations.

The problem represents two sides of the same coin: the passion most needed to breathe life into the body of Christ, is the force that most terrifies this male-dominated structure. It is the woman-love passion that is most needed, and is most feared. It is perceived as a touchy, feely, sensuous uncontrollable emotion that so vastly differs from the controlled rigidity which characterizes contemporary conservative Christianity, and which society applauds as manly. This masculinist structure is more terrified by any connection to a feminine force, perceived as fraught with suspicion, deceit, and Eve-connected feminine wiles. But Christ Himself describes His Church as His Bride, bringing into focus the level of intensity and passion that is expected of those who call themselves by His Name, and are expected to represent the manifestation of His Presence.

The romantic relationship between Jesus Christ and His people, is not a distant, scripted, bookish, theoretical love, but a searing, passionate love that cuts through traditions, customs, prejudices (race/ethnicity, class, colour, gender, age, national origin, political affiliation) and our own stubborn Adamic natures like a sharp knife through hot butter. It mirrors His own passionate love for His Father that led Him to shed His blood, willingly, for our Salvation. It is a fall-flat-on-our-faces love when convicted in sin; a jump- for-joy, David-like dance when blessed with His miraculous bounty; a luxurious laughter that accompanies the inner peace and confidence of dependence on a mighty and magnanimous God. It is not the stiff, structured and regulated love, so packed with propriety that passion, the fundamental representation of love, escapes. But human love is not perfect. Only Divine love is. And this is where our tolerance, patience and forgiveness play major roles. *Compassion must rule.*

In a sermon titled "Christ in You, the Hope of Glory," delivered at the Seventh Annual Retreat for Women at the Sligo Adventist Church in Maryland, Pastor Hyveth Williams talks of the spiritual romance that is necessary for a pure, undiluted intimacy with God for which women yearn. It is a love, according to Dr. Williams, that incorporates three kinds of love in the unconditional Agape love that Christians claim so casually. *Fileo* or brotherly/sister love that causes us to look out for and take care of each other, canceling all socially constructed barriers, such as race/ethnicity, colour, class, ***gender***, age, national origin or political affiliation; *eros*, or the kind of romantic and passionate love that we tend to associate with sexual sin, but actually embodies the fiery passionate love that, coupled with the *fileo* loves, fuels active involvement against discrimination and social injustice. My husband, for example, teases me about being a serial radical looking for a cause. It may be funny, but that is *eros*. Still the wily and erratic *eros* must be carefully directed to be effective. It is the chief ingredient of purposeful and aggressive action that transforms when the normal response is to conform. It is the nub of Christian love for God and for each other, which comes up missing in contemporary Christianity, causing us to submit to structure at the expense of substance. In the words of Pastor Williams: "We have lost *eros*. We have so much *Agape* that we are all filled with Heaven and can't do any good on earth." Another rarely acknowledge aspect of this *Agape* love is *storge* love, a glue-like love that lasts through life's daily bumps and grinds. It is dramatically related in the story of Ruth and Naomi, two women of substance, who exemplify a sisterly love that is over-the-top, while serving as a shining light. ***Ruth (1-4).***

It is not that these three characteristics which embody unconditional Agape love are naturally inherent in woman-love. But, drawing on the "Men are from Mars, Women are from Venus"[35] concept, it must remind us of the fundamental differences in women and men that logically carry over into woman-love and man-love. For John Gray, the author of this concept, the pervasive dishar-mony in male/female relationships is more than a clue that women and men want more...but more significantly,

---

35   John Gray, Ibid.

that the world needs more. In his sequel to this popular book, Gray continues:

> Through mastering the secrets of passion and practicing forgiveness, we are not only creating a lifetime of love for ourselves, but we are making a difference in the world. Practicing new relationship skills and learning to harmonize dissonant values is not only the prerequisite for creating more passionate relationships, but directly contributes to a more peaceful world.[36]

Indeed for Gray, it is through an awareness of our differences that we can overcome conflict and develop and activate "a new awareness that respects and harmonizes differences." (p262). Could it be that the whole Christian experience has been deeply influenced by the different ways in which men love, at the risk of marginalizing women's nurturing love? Has the Church then suffered from the failure to emphasize and/or include this nurturing woman-love that produces this sense of community? How could we indeed have a true community that sidelines the very essence of more than one half of that community? And more critically, has the word **religion**, then, come to take on more importance than the **relationship** on which the belief is based? Have we become more preoccupied with king-making than Kingdom-building? More **religious** than **real**? How do we put into our relationship with Christ, the pure passion that brands us and those whose lives we touch with His all-encompassing love? How can we place, maintain and sustain the passion into our compassion? *Stay passionate!*

The challenge, then, is to devise strategies for removing the frame from Eve to display God's mercy, bounty, and glory through Christ's passionate blood, shed for women and for men. It is an outrageous love and undeserving

---

36   John Gray, *Mars and Venus Together: Relationship Skills for Lasting Love* (New York: HarperCollins, 1996).

grace that flood, cleanse and bless, for purposeful action, the lives of women as well as men. Perhaps, just perhaps, even more so the lives of women. It demands a different perspective, a new initiative, indeed a new imperative, if we, as women and men of God, are to respond faithfully and fervently to the new and different challenges in these end times. It calls for an honest re-examination of the structures with which we have imprisoned Eve, in spite of the fact that she, too, has been washed and cleansed with the redemptive powers of a Resurrected Christ, and named for life itself. It requires a re-thinking of Mary's obedience to her awesome Call as counterpoint to Eve's disobedient action. Moreover, we must openly confront the ways in which these attitudes have slowed or outright hampered women's God-created purpose of collaboration as helpmeets.

There is need then to jettison old ideas and baggage that weigh us down as we seek to break through barriers, remove old frames, think outside the box, bolt out of the kitchen and soar beyond man-made restrictions to God-inspired designs for our lives. We have to use the past as guideposts to future action, not as burdens to keep us mired in traditions that stymie our individual and corporate growth. It is action as seen through the eyes of Christ Himself, who spurs us on: *"For my yoke is easy; and my burden is light." (Matthew 11:30, KJV)*. It is indeed time to remove time-worn beliefs that continue to fail Christ's Mission and Purpose to prepare for a new dispensation and a renewed vision. The Mission and Purpose include a deeper relationship of equality and mutuality between women and men for a more intimate relationship with God, in order to fulfil His purpose. If not now, then when? Will we continue to side-step, side-line, marginalize, misread and misinterpret the core of His message…that of an unequivocal Agape love which binds us, women and men together, as we soar onwards and upwards to His Higher Calling?

It is within this imperative that we must place the pervasive charges against the Christian Church and its doctrines as key to the problems which abused women confront. This returns us to one of the central concerns of this book. The male-dominated leadership in the Church that has been charged—in worst case scenarios—as accomplice to society in its wanton disregard for women and women's issues, and its tacit support or failure to address domestic violence or family violence in all of its myriad forms. Just think for a minute: How many times have you heard an entire sermon preached on domestic violence? Domestic violence has become an international *cause celebre*, with global recognition of its human rights violation that affects not only children and families, but whole communities and nations. Afghanistan is only the nation *de jour*. A startling majority of Western women languish in repressive structures that have similar consequences, though different in style and degree of intensity and visibility.

Let's not forget the ugly facts noted in Chapter 1: In the United States and Canada, 31% of all women killed are murdered by their husbands, ex-spouses or boyfriend. More than 504,400 women in the United States are stalked by an intimate partner each year. Violence occurs in 28% of all marriages. Domestic Violence is now recognized as the Number One health threat to U.S. women, causing more injuries than automobile accidents, muggings and rapes combined. One-third of pregnant women are battered throughout pregnancy. Only about one-seventh of all domestic assaults are brought to the attention of the police. Youth are not immune: one in three teenagers are victims of dating abuse. Child abuse occurs in 70 percent of families that experience domestic violence, and domestic violence is one of the major causes of pre-natal death and injury. The elderly are equally vulnerable: one million people 65 years or older are victims of abuse each year. In nearly nine out of ten incidents of domestic elder abuse and neglect, the perpetrator is a family member. Domestic violence indeed includes violence against men, but according to the U.S. Department of Justice, 85% of victims of intimate partner abuse are female. The cost of family violence in the U.S. is $5 billion annually, including medical expenses, police and court costs, and loss of productivity in the work place. The global picture is equally horrifying: one out of three women has been beaten, coerced into sex, or otherwise abused. According to a 1997 UNICEF report, "Millions of women, in every country, on every continent, and of every class, live under the daily threat of physical abuse."[37] War-torn countries, in which women and children are kidnapped, raped, and kept as sex slaves represent the sordid end game of women's subjugation and violence against women.

> Rape is one of the most common and frequent of crimes against women in India. It has many forms: "landlord rape;" rape by those in authority of women employees or juniors within the workplace; "marital rape;" "caste rape" in which caste hierarchy is exercised to rape lower-caste or tribal women; "class rape;" "police rape;" and army rape."[38]

Wives are encouraged to subordinate themselves to their husbands in traditional Cambodian culture.

> Consequently, police only intervene when the woman is severely injured or killed and family and neighbors often will not provide protection or support to a battered woman. In fact, if a woman finds the inner strength to seek safety by escaping from her spouse, her efforts will

---

37 Leni Marin, Helen Zia and Esta Soler, ed., *Ending Domestic Violence: Report From the Global Frontlines* (San Francisco, California: The Family Violence Prevention Fund).

38 Ibid.

be impeded by Cambodian law, which does not provide civil protection remedies and makes divorce extremely difficult. The result is that women often suffer beatings rather than confront law and tradition to stop the violence.[39]

According to the UNICEF report:[40]

...legislation against domestic violence has been enacted in 44 countries around the world. In many countries there is a range of intervention activities:establishment of shelter services and crisis counseling facilities; gathering of data and statistics to document the extent of the problem and the response of institions; training of judges, police, prosecutors, medical and health care providers, and social service workers to improve response; and public education on the seriousness of domestic abuse.

There is not one word on the response or intervention on the part of the Church. This is hardly surprising. In my own renewed Christian experience of 15 years, I have heard passing reference to domestic violence from the pulpit all of three times, only once with prayer for victims and abusers by the enlightened male pastor. How does the Church evangelize and spread the gospel in countries with traditions which hold as a cultural norm the violation of women's human rights, yet either ignore or refuse to address women's worldwide oppression and subjugation? It is no exaggeration to say that the Church has failed in its Divine role and responsibility to be the first line of defense of women's human rights. In fact, it is difficult to argue against the belief that the Church has in fact afforded the society a safe place to hide in its flagrant violation of the human rights of women and children. Could this failure of the Church to be a shield against women's pain, suffering

---

39   Ibid.
40   Ibid.

and human rights violations be directly related to its failure to fully integrate women's perspectives, sentiments and energy into its own leadership, policy-planning and implementation hierarchy?

> The Church needs to be looking at the gospel from a holistic standpoint to enable women, empower and properly train them because we look to the Church. The membership of the Church is close to 80 or 90 percent women and children, compared to men, so I often say this, and sometimes some male pastors have gotten offended, but the truth is that women are a major reserve in the Body of Christ. We see that most of the missionaries that go in the mission field are women, especially in Africa, most of the women who went to Africa, apart from the initial ones, were women, and still are women. So some women go out of the zeal that they have in their heart; and even if the Church is not willing to send them or release them, they still go and do the work of the Lord...So whether the church sends or not, if God speaks to women, women have a desire and a zeal to go where God sends them, much like the women who went to the tomb. Men were afraid, they were hiding, they were afraid to lose their lives, some of them even denied that they knew Christ. But it was the women who went and brought the news that He was risen. It was women to whom He first revealed Himself as the Risen Christ and the Resurrected Lord.
>
> —Pastor Annette Taylor
> Bethel Outreach Ministries
> Maryland/Liberia

As women seek answers to the question, **"Why Weepest Thou?"**...and we are weeping: for ourselves, our children, our Church, our communities, and yes, for our men. It is clear that we must take back the power granted us in the Bible to shake off the shackles of subjugation and violence: physical, verbal, psychological, emotional, financial, political, and yes, spiritual. In organizing the Pan African Christian Women's

Alliance (PACWA) in the U. S., Pastor Annette Taylor substantiates her argument supporting women's right to teach and preach the gospel by drawing attention to the presence of women in the upper room at Pentecost, before His Ascension. She points to the unutilized workforce in women, who are often "far more committed to the things of Christ than many men would be."

> Many times when people read the Scriptures, they misread the Scripture, and they think that the disciples were only 12 men. But there were 120 disciples, which included Jesus' mother, along with all the women that had walked with Him. And they were in that upper room. And when Jesus said: 'Don't leave until the Holy Spirit comes,' And they were in the upper room when the Holy Spirit came, and they were all baptized with the Holy Spirit to be witnesses unto Him. So the women were just as great a witness unto Jesus as the men were.
> —Pastor Annette Taylor
> Bethel Outreach Ministries
> Maryland/Liberia

Organizations such as The Pan African Christian Women's Alliance (PACWA) have currently over 36 nations in Africa and Europe, with women in evangelism, training women's leadership, training in prayer and the US-based Women of Global Action (WOGA), collaborating and networking to ensure the empowerment and encouragement of women. The commitment is to encourage and support individual and collective action.

We must, then, draw on the value and validation of our lives so dramatically and consistently exhibited in Jesus' Ministry for our God-given freedom. With compassion, yes, but with the firm knowledge that we are backed by His Word and His Divine example. We must not allow our eyes to be blinded, our ears to be deafened, our voices to be muffled, or our understanding to be misdirected. The battle cry lies within Jesus' next question: "Whom Seekest Thou?" For women, it is found in bursting through barriers to freedom guaranteed in the Word, and by the doctrine of the Resurrection that He ensured Martha understood. In spite of the external restrictions, the burden of responsibility rests on women to understand who we are in Him, in order to claim our Divine Rights, along with our Human Rights. The words of one female pastor merit repetition: **"I am whoThe Word says I am."**

My own Spirit-guided studying of The Word has brought me to this *Genderstanding* of Jesus to re-frame Eve; jettison her baggage to the foot of the Cross; and claim our Divine Rights and freedom in Him. My prayer is that you do the same, using Divine knowledge, wisdom and guidance to forward His Cause and His Course—not man's—and to hasten His Coming. Praise His Mighty Name! Hallelujah!

Genderstanding Jesus:
Questions for Reflection, Discussion and Action
Chapter 7

1). Has the Christian experience been deeply influenced by the way in which men love, at the risk of marginalizing women's nurturing love?

2). Has the Church then suffered from the failure to emphasize this nurturing woman-love that produces this sense of community?

3). How could we indeed have a true community that sidelines the very essence of more than half of that community?

4). Has the word "religion," come to mean more than the "relationship" on which the philosophy is based?

5). How can we remove the focus from King-making to Kingdom-building?

6). What are the lessons learnt from this reading?

7). What plans do you have for turning them into action?

NOTES

AFTERWORD

"Where Eagles Fly"[41]
by Pastor Hyveth Williams, Ph.D.

Morning had broken, yet the mist hugged the earth in a passionate embrace, defying the early sun's power to break its bewitching spell upon the land. The farmer, long acquainted with nature's ritual, seemed unaffected by the scenery as he trudged through the dew-sprinkled meadow toward the hills near his home. As he hiked along the path, he came upon a rather strange-looking egg in a nest that had evidently been dislodged from the limbs of the very tall tree under which it lay. Since he was in the business of raising chickens, the farmer was immediately intrigued by the size and shape of the egg, which he took home and placed in the incubator to be hatched with the other eggs.

It wasn't long before this strange-looking egg produced an even stranger-looking chick. Larger than the others, with a broad, white tail band, white wing patches, and feathers on its legs clear down to its toes, the chick had a

---

41   Hyveth Williams, "Where Eagles Fly," *Will I Ever Learn? One Woman's Life of Miracles and Ministry* (Hagerstown, Maryland: Review and Herald Publishing Association, 1996). "Where Eagles Fly" is a sermon first preached at the Boston Temple in 1989 by Pastor Hyveth Williams. This sermon has been a tremendous personal blessing, and I am extremely grateful to Pastor Williams for permitting me to share it with readers. While it was preached in an Adventist Church, it holds relevance and inspiration for all Bible-believing Christians, women and men, who are poised for flight to Higher Ground.

peculiar air about it. Though obviously a bird like the others, it took long strides and made peeping noises instead of walking and clucking like the other chickens.

Yes, it was undeniably different as it grew bigger and bigger, and more and more out of place among the other barnyard birds.

But the farmer decided to raise it like a chicken anyway. He fed that strange bird like a chicken, he treated it like a chicken, and he even called it a chicken. And since that was the only name the big bird ever knew, it began to think and act like a chicken. It moved its oversized feet awkwardly as it struggled to scratch the ground like a chicken. Although its beak was too big and clumsy to peck at the feed on the ground, that giant bird lowered its head with great determination to learn this skill. Sometimes it longed to preen its feathers like the other chickens, but soon discovered this was only one of many chicken things it would never master. Still, not wanting to be different from the others, that poor bird tried so hard to be like the chickens that by and by it no longer felt so out of place in the barnyard.

One day a visitor came to the farm and while walking through the barnyard he saw this strange-looking bird. Surprised, the visitor asked the farmer why he had an eagle living among his chickens. Well, the farmer replied, the bird may be an eagle, but it had learned to live, eat, and think like a chicken, and since that was all the life it knew, that's all it ever would be.

The visitor argued with the farmer. No creature created by God to fly in lofty places was beyond redemption, no matter how long it had been confined to a barnyard. He said, "This bird may have the habits of a chicken, it may walk and squawk like a chicken, but deep inside it has the heart of an eagle." Determined to prove his point, he picked up the eagle, held it aloft, and said, "You're an eagle—spread your wings and fly!"

The eagle flapped its large, graceful wings, stretching those majestic pinions that lifted him, soaring toward the sky. The farmer began making clucking sounds and threw some chicken feed on the ground. When the eagle saw this, he flew right back to the ground and started to eat. Though the farmer gloated over his success, the visitor never gave up on the eagle.

Early the next morning he once more attempted to give the eagle a vision of its high calling. Taking it to the top of the barn, he pointed out the vast expanse of the beautiful countryside that was the bird's to explore as it discovered that a world existed far beyond the small barnyard. Again the visitor told the eagle that it was not a chicken, but a magnificent bird created by God to fly above the clouds. And again the eagle, now eager to discover its authentic identity, spread its wings and took off. Alas, as the bird ascended toward the sun, the farmer clucked like a chicken and threw some of its favourite chicken feed on the ground. But just as the eagle began to dive toward the feed, it heard the sound of another eagle calling in the distant sky.

The eagle's body trembled, pulsating with powerful energy as it hung almost suspended in midair, mesmerized by that haunting cry. With one great swoop, that majestic bird stretched its wings and soared toward the vast expanses of the great blue yonder. It flew up, up, up and away, slicing the air as it rose toward the dawning of a new experience. Not once did that eagle take a backward glance; not once did it look down as it soared effortlessly higher and higher toward the call of the other eagle, never to be a chicken again, but to live out its destiny where eagles fly!

Ephesians 2:1–5 presents a good description of chickens (which we all were at one time or another) before Christ came to our rescue. Even though God found us in desperate straits, He lifted us up to the level of His only begotten Son, whom He sent as the Visitor to redeem us from the barnyard of sin and deliver us to the safety of His Kingdom to live with God now and forevermore as the eagles He created us to be. Satan is like the farmer, and most of the time he captures Christians and brainwashes us into thinking we are chickens instead of eagles. We have the awesome challenge before us to be the catalyst of change, drawing youth and the elderly out of their obscure existence into a vibrant life with the Lord and His church. If you have been previously perceived as chickens, this is a warning to our observers that beginning today, we've begun to spread our wings and there's only one way to soar—up where we belong, where eagles fly!

The eagle is a familiar symbol in the Scriptures. Why does God single out this bird above all others to symbolize character traits He wants His people to embody? Perhaps because of its steadfastness, diligence, unswerving loyalty, and tender care for its young.

It is interesting to note that eagles are not as easily reproduced as chickens, and no matter how well-disguised, once an eagle, always an eagle. So it is with royalty. You may know the story of the prince and the pauper, in which the young prince swapped his royal throne and clothing for the rags of a street urchin. The prince sent him to take his place in the palace, while the young prince moved among the beggars and paupers to discover how he could better serve all the people in his kingdom. But no matter how hard he tried, or how tattered his dress, everyone who came in contact with him recognized that he did not belong among the beggars. He had a regal bearing, a peculiar air and speech that contradicted his shabby appearance. It was exactly that distinction that eventually revealed his secret and forced an end to his charade so that he had to return to his throne sooner than he planned.

According to *Philippians 2:5–8*, Prince Michael willingly chose to become Jesus Christ, the God-man, made lower than angels, a pauper, if you please, so that He could teach the poor in spirit and the slaves to sin how to live as princes in the kingdom of God. One of the most striking qualities that caused those who knew Jesus to be constantly amazed was His unique ability to present the familiar themes of God with authenticity and authority. People marveled because He did not speak like the scribes and Pharisees, but spoke with freshness and great wisdom, qualities that are quickly disappearing from among our people. Why? Perhaps because we've forgotten that we are princes and princesses of the royal household of God with all the rights and privileges to so live.

If anything marks us as chickens, it's our increasing inability to handle the great themes of the everlasting gospel with compassion and charity. We are content to sit on unique Adventist perches where we repeat meaningless mottos about having the truth and being the remnant, vain words that no longer have the power to convince ourselves, much less to convert those around us. We are fast becoming overpopulated with uniform birds of a feather who flock together once a week to pat our soft bellies, boast about our pointed beaks, and muse over our little heads that continue to hold fewer and fewer spiritual ideas and more and more philosophical ideologies. We've become chickens who are too chicken to take the risk for God and dare to be different. We desperately need keen-eyed, wide-winged creatures who are willing to soar where eagles fly, to explore the unlimited ranges of the kingdom of God. Jesus is asking us to be His eagles today. Will we?

Christian author Chuck Swindoll describes "eagle thinkers," who are very different from chicken people. Chicken people like to stay on the spiritual ground where it is safe, where they can feel the earth beneath their feet, earth carved out by the blood, sweat, and tears of risk-taking eagle pioneers. They like to pick over the same old feed and listen to the same old words, again and again, until they can follow the pattern by rote. They like to travel in groups, giving a little scratch here, or a little peck there from time to time, puling up an occasional worm. They can stay in the same yard, in the same rut, year after year, and I bet you can't remember the last time you saw a chicken fly. Chicken people are predictable, secure, boring, and as long as they have someone to throw a little feed to them at regular intervals, they are content with their lot. Most of the time they would rather starve or swallow junk than go out and find fresh food for themselves. They are always threatened by young, eager eagles who dare to spread their wings and fly.

If you want to know who the chickens in a church are, just listen to their complaints. They're the ones who are always disgruntled and critical because they seldom take the time to do more than scratch the surface of the Word of God. But not so the eagles. There's not a predictable pinion in their majestic wings! They love to think. They are driven by an inner urge to search, to discover, to learn. They are courageous, spiritually vibrant, tough-minded, willing to ask hard questions and perform intense, objective self-examination, bypassing the routine in pursuit of fresh, vigorous truth. Unlike the intellectually impoverished chicken, eagles take risks getting their food because they hate overprocessed food that is boring, repetitious, dry, and out of context with their personal experience and needs. When they encounter a problem, they come up with creative solutions.

An eagle-minded congregation would consider innovative approaches to combat the tide of disenchanted members. They would require consistent preaching of the gospel of Jesus Christ and practicing of the fundamental doctrines in the Bible. They would create aggressive programs that clearly announce that the church not only loves its young people, but cannot survive without them. An eagle-minded congregation would urge members to become involved with young people, applying the warmth of compassion rather than the whip of criticism to nurture them back into respected, full-fledged fellowship, so that they can cease to feel like they are chickens and dare to be eagles.

In every culture the eagle is recognized as a rare bird, a king of birds, a prized national emblem. Although the dictionary classifies the eagle as a large bird of prey, related to hawks, experts on birds identify the existence of only two species of eagles in North America: the golden and bald eagles. All other specie of eagles are said to be extinct. Chickens are so common they've never made the endangered species list. No matter how many chickens are killed for food or fun, they just keep on multiplying, while the eagle remains one of the most protected species in the animal kingdom. It is as uncommon and irreplaceable in its kingdom as you and I are in the kingdom of God. Perhaps that's why God so often uses the eagle as a symbol of His people, while the chicken, which represents those who rebel against Him, seems to multiply faster than we can count them. Furthermore, it is more likely for an eagle to think it is a chicken, and learn to live like one, than for a chicken to pass itself off as an eagle. And in spite of all its outstanding characteristics, it's much easier to shoot down an eagle than a chicken. That is why we need fewer chickens and more eagles on our religious skyline.

Another eagle quality to be emulated by God's people is its unlimited strength. Hans K. LaRondelle has written an impressive book entitled *Deliverance in the Psalms*. When he discusses Psalm 103:5, he points out that an eagle, unlike other birds, can live as long as 100 years and retain its vitality, youthfulness, and strength and be as fresh and vigorous on the day it dies as the day it winged its way from its mother's nest. Perhaps that's why Isaiah uses it as a symbol in chapter 40:28–31. No matter how wild the weather, an eagle can fly in the eye of the storm and is never smashed by the fierce winds against the rocks. It uses its great strength to rise high above the storm into clear, calm skies.

To be an eagle person means that you, too, possess the power to face the storms of life and rise above them. Storm clouds will always appear, and we cannot run from them. We must confront them in the strength of the Lord as we soar in the calm air of His presence. Eagle people take advantage of the rising air and the strong currents of opportunity that come with storms. They may be buffeted and beaten from all sides by raging winds, but still they can spread their gracious wings and glide above the torrents to find rest and peace in God. Being an eagle person may be a lonely experience. Not everybody understands eagle people. And what we humans don't understand, we fear. What we fear we attack, reject, or attempt to destroy.

In spite of all the threats, we are no longer chickens. Young people, you are no longer chicken. Little children, you are certainly not chickens. (**Women, you have never been chickens**).[42] All of us are eagles, created to spread our majestic wings and fly away from the common things into the sacred bosom of our loving Lord and be at rest. Not tomorrow, not soon, but now, today, while it is yet today! Now listen well, because I want you to hear what I am about to say. No amount of church going, hymn singing, long praying, religious talking, pious walking, or working for our salvation will put power into our wings so that we can fly away from the dark, deadly barnyard of this world where we are held captive. Only the call of God, heard through the preaching and teaching of His Word and relived in personal testimonies, individual devotions, and

---

42 Meryl James-Sebro's insertion and emphasis.

corporate Bible studies, can lift us up where we belong, where the eagles fly.

I once attended a boarding school in Jamaica. It was a Christian school, administered by a family from Scotland for the children of the rich and famous from around the world. Eventually the Jamaican government decided that some of its poor children should have an opportunity to enjoy the benefits and resources which, until then, had been exclusively reserved for wealthy foreigners. To gain entrance into this school, one had to pass a tough exam and win a scholarship. I was fortunate to be among the first 12 students to receive this prestigious opportunity.

I had the reputation even then of being very different from the rest of the crowd, someone who was not afraid to take risks, even if such risks resulted in the harshest punishment. One rule forbade those of us who didn't have straight hair to use hot combs to straighten our hair, forcing us to wear it natural in an "Afro." There's nothing wrong with wearing one's hair natural, but this was long before the early 1960s when Afros became the symbol of what's Black and beautiful. So it was always embarrassing for me to have this huge, uncontrollable bush on my head while nearly everyone else had neat braids and bows.

At the beginning of each term our suitcases were thoroughly searched at registration time and all our silk underwear and straightening combs were confiscated as tools of the devil. I figured that if I took a dinner fork and heated it over one of the kerosene lamps in our dorm (we didn't have electricity yet), I could do a reasonable job of straightening my hair. One day while I was busily burning myself to death with one of these hot forks, the girls' dean caught me red-handed. I was sent to sleep in the basement for two weeks. What was so horrible about this punishment was that no one in their right mind ever ventured to walk alone in the basement at night because it was rumoured that vicious ghosts and hostile spirits roamed the place, seeking living souls on whom to vent their pent-up rage.

I was sent to sleep in that basement for two weeks, and I lived to talk about it! I didn't encounter a single ghost, hostile or friendly, during that time. At the end of my punishment everyone was eager to hear every detail of my "dungeon" experience. Of course, I was happy to oblige with spine-chilling tales of encounters with horrible spirits. One afternoon just as the sun was setting, I stood before a large group of girls seated on the steps of the girls' dorm, painting vivid word pictures of my struggles with the different spirits I'd met in the basement. The girls were hanging on my every word, every now and then screeching in fright, when the dean walked by.

"Hyveth, you will never amount to anything," she said. "You'll always have one sordid story or another to tell. Today it's about your experience in the basement. Maybe when you grow up it'll be about your exploits in prison. In any case, young lady, you'll never amount to anything!"

I was already striving for acceptance by lying, but when she said those words I was transformed from a young eagle, eager to soar among the possibilities of life, into a chicken who spent the following years barely scratching the surface of my true potential. Those words became a branding iron that seared into my subconscious mind to haunt me until Jesus rescued me. (As it turned out, I was told later that the dean was the one who spent time in prison for helping her family defraud the government out of thousands of dollars of scholarship funds.) I was driven to despair. I determined I would prove her wrong and win her approval by becoming somebody. But no matter how hard I worked, no matter how much I attained, I still heard the dean's voice saying that I'd never amount to anything. I drove myself harder every day, sometimes to the point of burnout, to make sure these words would never come true in my life. And after all that was done I still ended up being afraid I would never amount to anything.

Perhaps some of you are broken images of who you truly are and are haunted by negative self-messages echoing in the halls of your minds. No matter how well-dressed or well-educated we are, we've come with misgivings about ourselves, painfully aware of our inadequacies, bowed low by the storms of life, hostages of childhood experiences, broken by failed relationships, and disappointments in life. All seem to confirm that we were raised like chickens and that's what we'll always be. Some of you have been told on too many occasions, by parents and peers, teachers and preachers, that you are chickens until, unfortunately, you've come to believe and accept it.

But listen to what the Word of God says in Ephesians 2, verses 4 and 5: "But God, (emphasis supplied) being rich in mercy, because of His great love with which He loved us, even when we were dead in our transgressions, made us alive together with Christ (by grace you have been saved)," and called you eagles, made to reign with God in majesty, like princes ad princesses. You must not settle for anything less. You must not allow the meanness, the jealousy, others' lack of vision to make you chickens. You are eagles! Get off your proverbial perch of self-pity and exchange the safety and comfort of your barnyard existence to soar, to explore the wide horizon of God's Word and will. As Pastor Swindoll says, eagles are awkward in barnyards and are awful misfits among chickens. They look pretty silly trying to pick over tasteless, dry feed on the ground when their beaks were made to tear into the living Word made flesh.

Let us, like the eagle, make our majestic flight above the clouds of spiritual mediocrity into the pure air of the Word of God. Let us soar with the spiritual eagles whom God has strategically placed around us to call us to higher planes where eagles fly. Let us soar up where we belong, where eagles fly!

*** *** ***

BIBLIOGRAPHY

The King James Version (KJV)

The New King James Version (NKJV)

The New International Version Study Bible (NIV)

The Clear Word Version (CWV)

Barker, Kenneth. *The NIV Study Bible.* Grand Rapids, Michigan: Zondervan Publishing House.

Blanco, Jack. *The Clear Word: An Expanded Paraphrase of the Bible to Nurture Faith and Growth.* Hagerstown, MD: Review and Herald Publishing Association, 1994.

Chesler, Phyllis. *Woman's Inhumanity to Woman.* Thunder's Month, 2002.

Gray, John. *Mars and Venus Together Forever: Relationship Skills for Lasting Love.* New York: HarperCollins Publishers, 1994.

————. *Men are from Mars, Women are from Venus: A Practical Guide for Improving Communication and Getting What You Want in Your Relationships.* New York: Harper Collins Publishers, 1992.

Jakes, T.D. *God's Leading Lady: Out of the Shadows and into the Light.* New York: G. P. Putnam's Sons, 2002.

James-Sebro, Meryl. "What Women Need From Their Church." *Message* (March/April 1999).

————. *Flagwomen: The Struggle Against Domestic Violence in Trinidad and Tobago.* UMI Microform 3007926. Ann

Arbor, Michigan: Bell & Howell Information and Learning Company, 2001.

Karssen, Gien. *Her Name is Woman: 25 Women of the Bible.* Colorado: Navpress Publishing Group, 1977.

Reece, Colleen. *Women of the Bible.* Ohio: Barbour Publishing, Inc., 1998.

Seager, J. *The State of Women in the World Atlas.* London: Penguin Books, 1997.

Underwood, U. J. *Women in their Place: Does God Call Women?* New York: TEACH Services, Inc., 1990.

Williams, Hyveth. *Anticipation:Waiting on Tiptoes for the Lord.* Idaho: Pacific Press Publishing Association, 2000.

———. *When Will I Ever Learn?: One Woman's Life of Miracles and Ministry.* Maryland: Review and Herald Publishing Association, 1996.

Zaoude, Aster. "The Hard Path to Gender Equality." *Choices.* New York: United Nations Development Programme, March 2002.

*** *** ***